D0947435

EXILED IN THE WORD

Jerome Rothenberg & Harris Lenowitz

E X I L E D

IN THE WORD

Poems & Other Visions of the Jews
from Tribal Times to Present

WITH COMMENTARIES BY

JEROME ROTHENBERG

COPPER CANYON PRESS / 1989

Exiled in the Word is a re-working and re-presentation of material that originally appeared in *A Big Jewish Book*, published by Anchor Press / Doubleday, in 1978.

Copyright © 1978, 1989 by Jerome Rothenberg
All rights reserved

ISBN 1-55659-026-1
Library of Congress Catalog Card Number 89-61458

The publication of this book was supported by a grant from the National Endowment for the Arts.

Copper Canyon Press is in residence with Centrum at Fort Worden State Park.

This book is composed in Ehrhardt type by The Typeworks.

COPPER CANYON PRESS
Box 271, Port Townsend, Washington 98368

Pre-Face / 3

THE WAYS

A Book of Powers

The First, the Last: A Poem of Ezra / 17
From The Greater Hekhalot: A Cosmic Hymn / 18
Edmond Jabès: *From* Elya: Door II / 19
Moses de Leon: *From* The Great Holy Assembly: The Names / 20
From Sefer Raziel: Hymn / 21
Naftali Bacharach: A Poem for the Sefirot As a Wheel of Light / 22
Jackson Mac Low: 1st Light Poem / 26
Ishmael ben Elisha: *From* Shi'ur Koma: The Measure of the Body / 27
For the Beard of the Great Face: A Vision & Poem / 29
Isaac Luria: A Poem for the Small Face / 31
Isaac Luria: A Poem for the Shekinah on the Feast of the Sabbath / 33
From The Greater Hekhalot: The Door Keepers / 37
Tristan Tzara: Angel / 39
Moses of Burgos: *From* The Book of the Left Pillar / 40
David Meltzer: *From* Hero/Lil: The Third Shell / 42
From The Book Bahir: On the Nature of Evil / 46
Yosef ibn Abitur: The "Who?" of Ibn Abitur of Cordoba / 47

A Book of Worlds

Joseph Gikatilla: The Withdrawal, The Exile / 51
Nachman of Bratzlav: *From* The Torah of the Void / 52
Joseph Gikatilla: Nothing / 59
Franz Kafka: Fragment / 60

From The Book of Formation: 10 Countings, with Commentaries / 61

Albert Einstein: *E* / 62

Samaritan: The Ten Words of Creation / 63

Variations on Genesis / 63

From The Pirke de Rabbi Eliezer / 65

A Prologue to the Elements of Creation / 65

Yannai: Fire-Poem: "& Then an Angel of the Lord Appeared to Him in a Tongue of Fire" / 66

Eleazar ha-Kallir: Water-Poem: A Prayer & Invocation to the Prince of Rain / 67

From The Book of Mysteries: Rites for the Sun / 71

The Code of Day & Night / 74

Menorah / 76

Nathan of Gaza: Serpent / 77

Harris Lenowitz: The Wind   Two Trees   Men and Women / 78

Louis Zukofsky: The Iyyob Translation from "A-15" / 80

THE VISIONS

A Book of Beards

Gertrude Stein: *From* Patriarchal Poetry / 85

From The Book of Genesis: Akeda / 86

From The Testaments of the 12 Patriarchs / 88

A Prologue to the Works of Moses / 91

Eleazar ben Judah of Worms: The Image of Speech at Sinai / 91

From The Book of Exodus: Song of the Sea / 92

From The First Book of Samuel: After the Shamans / 95

Amos the Prophet: A Vision in the Voice of Yahveh / 97

Psalm 137: Exile / 99

Elijah & the Priests of Baal: In a Time of Famine / 101

From A Poem about Ashera: How She Goes to Bull God El to Seek a House for Baal Her Son / 107

From The Alphabet of Ben Sira: The Birth / 110

Meshullam the Great ben Kalonymos: A Poem for the High Priest, Sung
    Thereafter on the Day of the *Kippurim,* As He Was Celebrated
    Also in *The Wisdom of Ben Sira* / 114
From The Acts of Saint John: The Round Dance of Jesus / 116
A Poem for Bar Yoḥai / 121
The Great Lament / 124

A Book of the Wars of Yahveh

Rochelle Owens: *From* I am the Babe of Joseph Stalin's Daughter / 125
Jesus ben Hananiah: The Prophecy of Jesus ben Hananiah / 126
From Toldot Yeshu: The Magician / 127
Yehuda ben Idi: The Withdrawal of the Shekinah from Her Home in the
    Temple / 129
A Curse & Angry Poem Against the Nations / 130
Moses de Leon: *From* Midrash of the Absent: Messiah / 131
Abraham Abulafia: How He Went as Messiah in the Name of Angel Raziel
    to Confront the Pope / 133
The Rainbow Calendar of Isaac Luria / 134
"1648": For Cossacks / 136
Nathan of Gaza: *From* The Vision of Rabbi Abraham: The Birth &
    Circumstances of the Messiah Sabbatai Zevi / 137
3 Poems for Sabbatai Zevi the True Messiah as Drawn from Hymns Sung
    by His Faithful Followers after His Conversion to Islam for the
    Greater Glory of the God of Israel / 139
The Song of the Sexton / 141
Jacob Frank: *From* The Book of the Sayings of the Lord / 142
Five for the Rebbe / 147
Rajzel Zychlinska: Poor People / 149
Zaritsky's Children, & Other Poems for the Rich / 149
Peretz Markish: Two Poems / 151
Jacob Glatstein: Good Night, World / 153
Paul Celan: A Death Fugue / 154
Uri Zvi Greenberg: *From* God in Europe / 156
Yehuda Amichai: National Thoughts / 157

Allen Ginsberg: Jaweh and Allah Battle / 158
Jerome Rothenberg: Terror / 160
George Oppen: Semite / 164

THE WRITINGS

A Book of Writings

1

The Gezer Calendar / 169
YHVH's Battle with the Serpent / 170
The Song of Deborah / 171
From The Song of Songs / 175
The Maiden / 178
Hebrew: A Charm Against Lilith / 180
Yiddish: The Evil Eye (The Good Eye) Einehore / 181
Judeo-Arabic: Children's Rain Songs / 183
Arabic: Bride's Song Against Demons / 184
Yiddish: The Thief's Play / 185
Yiddish: Lullaby a Story / 188

2

Eleazar ha-Kallir: A Calendar: The Year of the Messiah / 189
Piyut: A Great Music / 194
Samuel ha-Nagid: Three Love Poems / 194
Solomon ibn Gabirol: The 16-Year-Old Poet / 196
Solomon ibn Gabirol: *From* Crown of Kingdom: The Constellations / 196
Judah ha-Levi, per Charles Reznikoff: *From* Jehuda Halevi's Songs to
        Zion / 197
Abraham ibn Ezra: "I Have a Garment" / 198
Isaac ben Abraham Gorni: Proensa / 199
Immanuel ben Solomon of Rome: Italian Sonnet / 200
Kalonymos ben Kalonymos: *From* Stone of Choice / 200

Maulana Sabin: *From* The Epic of King Kishvar: The Castle / 202

Israel ben Moses Najara: "Children of the Times" / 204

A Book of Extensions

Abraham Abulafia: *From* The Book of the Letter / 205

A Performance on the Great Name from the Eighth or Hidden Sacred
    Book of Moses Called "Unique" or "Holy" / 206

Isaac the Blind: "Lock Your Heart That It May Not Brood" / 209

Moses Cordovero: *From* The Garden of Pomegranates: The Unity of
    God / 210

Concrete Poem: YHVH Great God / 211

Moses Cordovero: Composition Around the Ineffable Name / 212

Name Event One / 213

Name Event Two / 213

Abraham Abulafia: *From* The Life of the World to Come / 214

Wallace Berman: *From* Image of the Wall / 220

The Masorah Calligrams / 221

Tristan Tzara: Calligram / 224

Jacques Gaffarel: Celestial Alphabet Event / 225

Moses Cordovero: The 10 Sefirot As a Labyrinth of Letters / 226

Maria Hebrea: The Numbers / 227

A Talisman for Venus / 228

Charlie Morrow: A Number Blessing / 229

25 Gematria / 230

Chance Composition No. 1 / 233

Chance Composition No. 2 / 233

Zohar Event: A Simultaneity for 10 or More Readers / 234

Tristan Tzara: *From* Manifesto on Feeble & Bitter Love / 234

Jackson Mac Low: Kaddish Gatha / 235

From The Havdala of Rabbi Akiba / 236

From The Babylonian Talmud: Signs / 238

From The Mishnah: Clean & Unclean / 239

Sounding Events / 241

Word Events / 243

Sound Event: The Silent Orchestra / 243
Allan Kaprow: Words / 243
Rain Event One / 247
Tree Spirit Events / 247
Nachman of Bratzlav: Vision Event / 248
A Scenario for Midnight / 249

Sources & Acknowledgments / 251

EXILED IN THE WORD

THE BAAL SHEM TOV used to go to a certain place in the woods & light a fire & pray when he was faced with an especially difficult task & it was done.

His successor followed his example & went to the same place but said: "The fire we can no longer light, but we can still say the prayer." And what he asked was done too.

Another generation passed, & Rabbi Moshe Leib of Sassov went to the woods & said: "The fire we can no longer light, the prayer we no longer know: all we know is the place in the woods, & that will have to be enough." And it was enough.

In the fourth generation, Rabbi Israel of Rishin stayed at home & said: "The fire we can no longer light, the prayer we no longer know, nor do we know the place. All we can do is tell the story."

And that, too, proved sufficient.

Pre-Face

Rabbi Eliezer said
     "prayer 'fixed'?
     "his supplication bears no fruit

. . . .

the question next came up: what
     is FIXED?
Rabba & Rabbi Yosef answered
     "whatever blocks the will
     "to MAKE IT NEW
                  (*Talmud*)

I

There was a dream that came before the book, & I might as well tell it. I was in a house identified by someone as THE HOUSE OF JEWS, where there were many friends gathered, maybe everyone I knew. Whether they were Jews or not was unimportant: I was & because I was I had to lead them through it. But we were halted at the entrance to a room, not a room really, more like a great black hole in space. I was frightened & exhilarated, both at once, but like the others I held back before that darkness. The question came to be the room's name, as if to give the room a *name* would open it. I knew that, & I strained my eyes & body to get near the room, where I could feel, as though a voice was whispering to me, creation going on inside it. And I said that it was called CREATION.

I now recognize that dream as central to my life, an event & mystery that has dogged me from the start. I know that there are other mysteries – for others, or for myself at other times, more central – & that they may or may not be the same. But CREATION – *poesis* writ large – appeared to me first in that house, for I was aware then, & even more so now, that there are Jewish mysteries that one confronts in a place no less dangerous or real than that abyss of the Aztecs:

    ... a difficult, a dangerous place, a deathly place: it is dark, it is light ...

& with a sense too that this space must be bridged, this door opened as well – the door made just for you, says the guardian in Kafka's story. Yet

Kafka, like so many of us, poses the other question also: "What have I in common with Jews? I have hardly anything in common with myself. . . . "

For myself it had suddenly seemed possible – this was in 1966 or '67 & I was finishing *Technicians of the Sacred* – to break into that other place, "my own . . . a world of Jewish mystics, thieves, & madmen." From that point on, it opened up in stages. Images, once general & without particular names, now had identified themselves. I let my mind – & the words of others, for I had learned as well to collage & assemble – work out its vision of "fantastic life," as Robert Duncan had called it for all poetry: an image in this instance of some supreme yiddish surrealist vaudeville I could set in motion. With those poems (*Poland/1931*) I made a small entry, American & eastern European; yet something had dropped away, so that it was now possible to be "in common with myself," to experience the mystery of naming, like the thrill & terror of my Jewish dream.

Still the event wasn't "mine" but part of a process of recovery in our time, of the "long forbidden voices" invoked by Whitman over a century ago, the "symposium of the whole" set forth in Duncan's "rites," now pulling all our impulses together:

> . . . The female, the proletariat, the foreign; the animal and vegetative; the unconscious and the unknown; the criminal and failure – all that has been outcast and vagabond must return to be admitted in the creation of what we consider we are. (R.D.)

And the Jew too among the "old excluded orders," not in the name of "the incomparable nation or race, the incomparable Jehovah in the shape of a man, the incomparable Book or Vision," but come into "the dream of everyone, everywhere." A primal people, then, as instance of those cultures of the old worlds, built through centuries of preparation, not to be repeated, whose universality arises, like all others, from its own locations, its particulars in space & time.

The work of many, poets & others, has gone into that process, both inventing & re-inventing – the Jewish side of which turns up for us in contemporaries like Celan, Hirschman, Jabès, Meltzer, Owens, Tarn, as well as others, friends or enemies, who struggle with that Jewish daemon, force us to renew, to make again, the statement of the great refusal. Jewish, human at the core.

2

The work, as set out here, includes both terms: the Jewish & the human. In that second, larger frame – of which the first is, for myself, a central & sufficient instance – the matters that touch on the "recovery" are, first, the idea of *poesis* as a primary human process; second, the primacy of the "oral tradition" in *poesis;* third, the re-invigoration of the bond between ourselves & other living beings; fourth, the exploration of a common ground for "history" & "dream-time" (myth); & fifth, the "re-invention of human liberty" (S. Diamond) in the shadow of the total state.[1] These are the keys to any "modernism" still worth its salt. And they are the keys also to the oldest poetry we know: that of the shaman-poets, "technicians of the sacred," whose visionary use of song & speech had its roots, by every mark we've learned to read, back into the Old Stone Age. And it was just this poetry, this language-of-vision in a culture that was communalistic, anarchic, & egalitarian, that the newer city-states tried to destroy, no less in Judaea – where the cry was "thou shalt not suffer a shaman to live" – than in other civilizations throughout the world.

The poet, if he knows his sources in the "sacred actions" of the early shamans, suffers anew the pain of their destruction. In place of a primitive "order of custom," he confronts the "stony law" & "cruel commands" Blake wrote of – "the hand of jealousy among the flaming hair." Still he confirms, with Gary Snyder, the presence of a "Great Subculture . . . of illuminati" within the higher civilizations, an alternative tradition or series of traditions hidden sometimes at the heart of the established order, & a poetry grudgingly granted its "license" to resist. No minor channel, it is the poetic *mainstream* that he finds here: magic, myth, & dream; earth, nature, orgy, love; the female presence the Jewish poets named Shekinah.

In the Jewish instance – as my own "main main" – I can now see, no longer faintly, a tradition of *poesis* that goes from the interdicted shamans (= witches, sorcerers, etc., in the English Bible) to the prophets & apocalyptists (later "seers" who denied their sources in their shaman predecessors) & from there to the merkaba & kabbala mystics, on the right hand, & the gnostic heretics & nihilist messiahs, on the left.[2] But I don't

---

1. By *poesis* I mean a language process, a "sacred action" (A. Breton) by which a human being creates & re-creates the circumstances & experiences of a *real* world, even where such circumstances may be rationalized otherwise as "contrary to fact." It is what happens, e.g., when the Cuna Indian shaman of Panama "enters" – as a landscape "peopled with fantastic monsters & dangerous animals" – the uterus of a woman suffering in childbirth & relates his journey & his struggle, providing her, as Lévi-Strauss tells it, "with a language by means of which unexpressed or otherwise inexpressible psychic states can be immediately expressed." This "power of the word," while often denied or reduced to posturings or lies in the "higher" civilizations, has continued as a tradition among poets & others who feel a need to "express the inexpressible" (see below, page 18) – a belief in what William Blake called "double vision" or, in Lévi-Strauss's paraphrasing of Rimbaud, that "'metaphor' can change the world."

2. This follows roughly the stages (torah, mishna, kabbala, magic & folklore, etc.) by which the "oral tradition" ("torah of the mouth") was narrowed & superseded by the written. But not without resistance; says the *Zohar:* "The Voice should never be separated from the Utterance, & he who separates them becomes dumb &, being bereft of speech, returns to dust." An ongoing concern here.

equate it with mysticism *per se* ("which appears to love a mystery as much outside as it does in," writes Charles Olson), rather prize it in every break through of "poetic mind" – that drive to *make it new* (E. Pound), to pit the old transformative ways of thought against the other, intervening drive toward an authoritative written text &, what confronts us once again, the reduction of particulars to what has become the monoculture. I would expect it, as much as anywhere else, in the secular poets of our own time, even or most particularly those who resemble what Gershom Scholem calls "nihilist mystics," for whom "all authority is rejected in the name of mystical experience or illumination" & who leap, like Rimbaud's seer-poet, "into the unknown" – the "cauldron" Scholem names it, place of "promiscuity," etc., "in which the freedom of living things is born." Separated from mysticism, *poesis* persists as process, as preparation: it is evolving, contradictory, not fixed or rigid but "with an infinite capacity for taking on new forms." The poet meets the mystic where "their end, their aim" – wrote Moses Porges, 1794 – "is liberation from spiritual & political oppression."

Now, all of this I would have stressed in any approach to the development of *poesis* in the "West" – an area I deliberately avoided when I was first compiling *Technicians of the Sacred.* Before coming to the idea of what I came to call "a big Jewish book," I had in fact played with the possibility of a pan-European gathering. But that seemed too diffuse for present purposes, & I thought to speak instead from the Jewish instance, which, through diaspora, would still touch all bases, European & more than European – & from an idea too that the specific & even local circumstances (of which I was certainly a part) provided the most direct line for poetic vision. In its Jewish form, then, I could isolate a series of topics & conflicts, tensions, that were either unique or more developed there than elsewhere, or that were developed with concrete, often "dramatic" particulars that formed a hedge against "abstraction" & mere "objectivity." While most turn up in the texts & commentaries below, there are a few I would stress as those that hold me to the Jewish work:

- a sense of exile both as cosmic principle (exile of God from God, etc.) & as the Jewish fate, experienced as the alienation of group & individual, so that the myth (gnostic or orthodox) is never only symbol but history, experience, as well;

- from which there comes a distancing from nature & from God (infinite, ineffable), but countered in turn by a *poesis* older than the Jews, still based on namings, on an imaging of faces, bodies, powers, a working out of possibilities (but, principally, the female side of God – Shekinah – as Herself in exile) evaded by orthodoxy, now returning to astound us;

• or, projected into language, a sense (in Jabès's phrase) of being "exiled in the word" – a conflict, as I read it, with a text, a web of letters, which can capture, captivate, can force the mind toward abstract pattern or, conversely, toward the framing, raising, of an endless, truly Jewish "book of questions";

• &, finally, the Jews identified as mental rebels, who refuse consensus, thus become – even when bound to their own Law, or in the face of "holocaust," etc. – the model for the Great Refusal to the lie of Church & State.

And it's from such a model – however obscured by intervening degradations from *poesis*, impulse to conform, etc. – that I would understand the Russian poet Marina Tsvetayeva's dictum that "all poets are Jews."

3

If this keeps me attached to the "history of the Jews" & identified with it, I realize too that the terms in which I present it often go beyond what has seemed reasonable to those living within it. Like other peoples with a long history of life under the gun, Jews have tended in their self-presentation (whether to themselves or others) to create an image that would show them in the "best light" & with the least possibility of antagonizing their oppressors. By doing so we have often denied ourselves the assertion of a full & multi-sided humanity, choosing to present an image that was gentle, passive, sensitive, & virtuous, & that in its avoidance of complication tended to deny negative emotions or experiences & to avoid claims to ideas & personalities that our antagonists had staked out as their own. This was further assisted by the circumscriptions of Jewish orthodoxy, with its concept of the single immutable vision & text, & with its hostility to innovators & counter-culturists among its own people. For many Jewish poets & artists, working within a Jewish context came to mean the surrender of claims to the sinister & dangerous sides of existence or to participation in the fullest range of historical human experience. In the process many came to confuse the defensive or idealized image with the historical & to forget that the actual history of the Jews was as rich in powers & contradictions as that of the surrounding nations.

Once into this book, it also seemed to me that much that I had taken for granted about the Jewish past – & present – no longer held up. Since such discoveries influenced my further work, even as I made them, I think I should present some of them here – or present them (for economy) along with a series of statements on the sources & boundaries of this book.

As supreme wanderers – even before & after the forced disaspora – the Jews' historical & geographical range has been extraordinary. To map this some years ago in *A Big Jewish Book*, I included works from the ancient Jewish languages – Hebrew & Aramaic – & from those like Yiddish & Ladino developed in the course of exile, as well as from other languages (Greek, Arabic, German, English, Persian, French, etc.) used by Jews in biblical & post-biblical times. But I remain impressed as well by the continuity of a specifically Hebrew poetry which, far from being stifled in the aftermath of "Bible," produced a series of new forms & visualizations, the diversity of which is in itself a matter of much wonder.

Alongside this continuity, there are three turning points in the history of Jewish consciousness that I would stress here:

- a shift, early along, from both the older shamanism & the general pattern of ancient Near Eastern religion to the centralized & gradually dominant monotheism of the Priests & Prophets;

- a series of changes around the time of Jesus (but really from a century or two before to a century or two after), in which the Jews – as a *large* & mobile population,[3] scattered throughout the Mediterranean & maintaining an active poetic & religious tradition in both Hebrew & Greek – generated a number of conflicting movements: christian & gnostic on the one hand, rabbinic, messianic, & kabbalistic on the other;

- with the triumph of Church & Synagogue, the entry of Jewish consciousness into an extraordinary subterranean existence that would erupt later in a series of libertarian movements: within a Jewish frame, the 17th- & 18th-century Sabbateans & Frankists, 20th-century Zionists, etc., & outside it the critical role of Jews & ex-Jews in revolu-

---

3. Recent estimates for the 1st century B.C. set the Jewish population as high as 8 million, thus 6–9% of the Roman Empire, 20% of the eastern provinces, 33% of Alexandria, etc. (Michael Grant, *The Jews in the Roman World*, page 60, plus relevant sections in Louis Finkelstein, *The Jews: Their History, Culture, & Religion.*) And prior to their later defeat & subjection, the Jews were also heavily into conversion – both full & partial – & "almost uniquely among the subjects of Rome ... were still producing an extensive literature of their own." (M. Grant.)

tionary politics (Marx, Trotsky, etc.) & avant-garde poetics (Tzara, Kafka, Stein, etc.).

(That we are now in a fourth phase – post-Holocaust & including the settlement of Israel & the Palestinian disaster – may mark the termination of the Jewish dream & possibility set forth in these pages.)

Work for this book has accordingly been drawn from both "sacred" & "secular" sources, with the link between them *my* stress on a poetic/visionary continuum & on the mystical & magical side of the Jewish tradition. And since poetry, in the consensus of my contemporaries, is more concerned with the "free play of the imagination" than with doctrinal certainties *per se,* I've made no attempt to establish an "orthodox" line or to isolate any one strain as purer or more purely Jewish than any others. Instead my assumption has been that poetry, here as elsewhere, is an inherently impure activity of individuals creating reality from all conditions & influences at hand.

Concretely this non-doctrinal approach has called for attention to sources like the following, many not usually found in such a gathering:

 • tribal & polytheistic remnants, like the battle of Yahveh & the Sea Serpent, the story of Lilith, the accounts of angels, etc. as the Sons of God, even Ugaritic (Canaanite) narratives of Baal & Ashera, etc.;

 • non-canonical & "heretical" texts, viewed as a subterranean continuation of the earlier traditions – but principally celestial spirit journeys & power dreams in the work of merkaba & apocalyptic visionaries; this includes both acknowledged apocrypha (4th Book of Ezra, Book of Enoch, etc.) & more heterodox texts like *Sefer ha-Hekhalot* (Book of Palaces), "The Code of Day & Night" from the Dead Sea Scrolls, etc.;

 • visionary poetry of early Jewish Christians & Gnostics, including New Testament works like the Book of Revelation (not presently included), & gnostic ones like the "Round Dance of Jesus" in the Acts of Saint John or those of messianic figures like Simon Magus, etc.; also antichristian writings like the *Toldot Yeshu* counter-gospel;

 • kabbala, as the last great oral (thus: secret, whispered) tradition of ancient Judaism, leading from 2nd-century mystics like Simeon bar Yoḥai & Ishmael ben Elisha to the *Zohar* of Moses de Leon, the discourses & mystic hymns of Isaac Luria, the "abstract" graphics of Abulafia & Cordovero, the later messianic heresies of Sabbatai Zevi & Jacob Frank, etc.;

- the Jewish magical tradition, in all its manifestations, as a poetry of naming & invocation: ancient texts like the 3rd-century *Sefer ha-Razim* (Book of Mysteries), magical texts in the recognized kabbala & in "spurious" classical & medieval works like the "Book of Moses on the Secret Name," & later oral & folkloristic traditions in Hebrew, Yiddish, Arabic, etc.;

- the poetry of Jewish groups outside the European &/or rabbinical "mainstream": Essenes, Samaritans, Karaites, Falashas, Chinese Jews, etc.;[4]

- previously downgraded figures like the medieval *paytanim*, liturgical poets whose poems (*piyutim*) have remained in prayer books but long been ignored or ridiculed in favor of the more literary & "classical" Hebrew poets of Spain, etc., though many of the latter are shown as well;

- the work of later Jewish poets, even where it develops into an apparently "anti-Jewish" point of view. (Here the proliferation in our time & place of the Jewish side of *poesis* is itself a point worth making – not only as theme [ancestral poetry, etc.] but in the energy of a large number of poets [Stein, Zukofsky, Tzara, Ginsberg, Mac Low, etc.] who have been central to the "real work of modern man: to uncover the inner structure & actual boundaries of the mind" [G. Snyder].)

While such sources show some of the ways in which I've tried to break new ground, much of the older matter in the book has in fact been drawn from the generally accepted literature (Bible, Mishna, Talmud, Zohar, etc.) & from poets for whom the problem of "identity" probably never arose. But even here my intention was to stress process over the mere re-statement of earlier ideas (the poem not as a "'fit' but a unification of experience" – William Carlos Williams) & to return to a sense of the original moment, renewing the poetic event by all means of interpretation (translation) at my disposal. Thus, visionary & dream accounts in the prophetic books have been retranslated to emphasize the immediate experience, or the very ancient Song of Deborah has been treated as an oral performance piece or re-enactment by a poet-singer who assumes a range of roles & voices. And, as much here as elsewhere, I have tried to show the many sides of Jewish

4. Some works mentioned here were included in *A Big Jewish Book* but do not appear in *Exiled in the Word*.

experience, including instances (e.g., the gloating over Sisra's death in "Deborah," etc.) that went against my grain but revealed some part of the reality.

As in *Technicians of the Sacred*, I have also worked by analogy with contemporary forms of poetry & art, to isolate structures not usually included in the conventional anthologies or not thought of as poetry *per se.* The most striking of these are the many types of language happenings that form the "mantric" base of traditional Jewish mysticism & kabbala: "masoretic" visual poems; word-events used in the transformation of older texts &/or in the creation & discovery of the names of God; sound-poems arising from that process or in the wordless chanting of religious celebrants, etc. In addition, various ritual forms have been treated, where relevant, in the manner of intermedia events & happenings, & because of the book's range ("from tribal times to *present*") have been presented alongside contemporary artists & poets like Kaprow & Mac Low. Such inclusions have reinforced my sense that both a contemporary critique of "civilization" & a concern with experimental, often non-ikonic forms of language have a particular resonance & an actual history within the Jewish context.

4

I have seen the work of this book as itself an act of *poesis:* the creation – from all conceivable sources & attempts at definition – of "a big Jewish book," a composition & collage that would project my vision of the Jewish mysteries. That intention has determined the structure of the book as a whole. In brief, then, my first decision as to structure was to stress idea over author, or, by a non-chronological arrangement, to play up the relationship between older work & very contemporary developments in poetry, particularly those practiced in the U.S. over the past few decades. (I would have done the same for any work with such a time-scale.) The model for the present gathering is in fact the "big Jewish book" par excellence, the *Bible:* an anthology (some, even in that instance, would say "collage") whose common name in Hebrew (*TaNaKh*) is an acronym based on its three traditional divisions: *Torah* (or "Law"), *Neviim* (or "Prophets"), & *Khtuvim* (or "Writings"). With this in mind I worked out a similar three-part structure into Ways, Visions, & Writings, & a movement from myth to history to language & poetics *per se.*

Thus, the opening, *Ways* (a designation derived from the equation by the Chinese Jews in K'ai-fêng of torah & tao – plus my own urge toward the plural), begins with a "Book of Powers" that explores both old & new attempts to name & describe the "unnameable" & "ineffable" god of the traditional religion, as well as the other beings & domiciles associated with that ancient reality concept; & it moves in its second part to a "Book of Worlds," or the attempts to give an image to the process of creation & the phenomena it generates. (These two "books" correspond to the "Work of the Chariot" & the "Work of Creation" of the merkaba mystics.)

The second major section, *Visions*, moves from "myth" to "history" & plays between visionary experience in its dream-time aspects & visionary experience as the attempt to locate or to re-locate ourselves in space & time. It is again divided into two "books": an older section or "Book of *Beards*" (the literal Hebrew word for Patriarchs or Elders), whose order of events, though not of composition, goes from "patriarchal" Abraham to the first openings & losses in the time of Jesus; & a later section called "A Book of the Wars of Yahveh," in which the theme of exile (seen cosmically in "Powers" & "Worlds") takes on a desperate new meaning in the life of individual & nation, & in which the implied hero is the dangerous messiah-poet (Jesus is only the best-known instance) who asserts the possibilities of freedom in a world of "cruel commands" & spiritual withdrawals.

The final major division of the book, *Writings*, continues much of this imagery, etc., but here the focus is on the forms of both the written & the spoken language in a culture presumably dominated by "the book," yet permeated as well by the idea of an oral tradition that underlies & brings the written word to life. To explore this even minimally a two-part division again seemed necessary, into a "Book of Writings," mapping high points of Jewish *poesis* (anonymous & oral first, then written) from the time of the Gezer Calendar (10th century B.C.) to the work of pre-modern Jewish poets in a range of languages & cultures, & an accompanying "Book of Extensions," dealing with the recovery of forms of language & "language happenings" that our conventional poetics had long ignored.

In addition I have used a variety of "commentaries" in a more extensive & sometimes more personal way than in my previous gatherings. I have tried to be judicious in the use of these, eliminating or depersonalizing them as the poems or sections seemed to demand. And along with the commentaries – & the dates & languages included in the titling of each translated text – I have appended a final section of "sources & acknowledgments," not only to identify where the material comes from but to keep the process of commentary & collage going until the very end. I suppose, finally, that this tendency to uninterrupted discourse is itself a part of the Jewish "oral tradition": a tradition which, at its best, recognizes the double origins of *poesis* in song & speech, its survival to address a silent God & universe.

5

> So, with God dead, I found my Jewishness confirmed in the book, at the predestined spot where it came upon its face, the most grieved, the most unconsoled, that man can have.
> Because being Jewish means exiling yourself in the word and, at the same time, weeping for your exile.
> — Edmond Jabès, *Elya*

The present version – coming more than a decade after *A Big Jewish Book* – is my attempt to present that work in a more compact form, while still not losing the sense of range that was part of its original reason-for-being. As before I hope that what emerges is an account of how poetry (& not just "Jewish" poetry) may function in a particular series of historical instances, not so much as a literary event but as related to the ways in which we experience & interact with the world in the most mundane & most elevated of human situations.

In condensing the book, I've been aware of some changes of emphasis, & I assume that others may have taken place outside my immediate awareness. There is proportionately more of the past here than before, although I've attempted again to see that past "from the point of view of the present." I've also made some additions or substitutions, but in either case my choice has been to keep certain key issues alive & to use the assemblage as much as I could to unfold a kind of (Jewish/human) myth or story. The balance between orthodox & heterodox (as central to that story) has undoubtedly shifted – in some sections more toward the one, in others toward the other. And in spite of a relative diminishing of the "gnostic" & the marginally Jewish, I feel a stronger presence than before of the heretical & the formerly suppressed – at least that I've favored the rarely seen over the patently familiar, wherever such a choice had to be made.

The decade that followed the publication of *A Big Jewish Book* carried the Jewish story forward, but with twists, as many of us saw it, that turned the myth of exile on its head. In my own work as a poet, I found myself returning – over whatever distance it by now involved – to the terror of the holocaust that brought the exile of the Jews to an end, while it changed the sense of the human that informs the poetics of this book & all that we meaningfully do as poets. Both in the new title of the book & in the arrangement of materials, *exile* has been foregrounded (along with language) as the work's main theme. Yet if this corresponds to a genuine fact of Jewish history, it is also present today in the tragedy of Palestine & (from a Jewish perspective) the irony of the *intifada* – of the resistance of a stateless people against the "Jewish state." It is my belief, spoken throughout these pages, that "exile" is central to our fate as humans, that it is political as much as spiritual, and that its corollary (once deeply Jewish) is a dream of liberation & a message, precisely, of *resistance*. It is this message that the book attempts to chart – as the kind of struggle that Jewish history & myth had so persistently explored until our time.

As such the book is dedicated to those who can most use it.

JEROME ROTHENBERG
San Diego
1976/1989

THE WAYS

Question. Is not the liturgical poet who first
writes that clay vessels in which leaven was
cooked must be broken before Passover, & then
states that they may be stored away in wooden
sheds, guilty of a contradiction?

Answer. It is poetic liberty to state together
two contradictory propositions.
                    — RABBI MEIR OF ROTHENBURG

I form the light & create darkness
I make peace & create evil
I Yahveh do all these things
                    — ISAIAH BEN AMOZ, THE SEER

A Book of Powers

(proem)   into the darkness of the jewish life   mysterious untamed   he enters   stars & jellies at the core   a substance I never had the grasp of   light is lightless   there is something before light   light is still to be created   journey deeper   light beneath the skull   before my birth   my mind

---

(Latin, from Hebrew/Greek, c. 100 A.D.)

THE FIRST, THE LAST   "A Poem of Ezra"

He said to me: In the beginning of the world
Before the gates of heaven stood
Before the blasts of thunder sounded
Before the flashes of lightning blazed
Before the foundations of Paradise were set
Before the beauty of its flowers was seen
Before the powers of the earthquake were laid down
Before the innumerable hosts of angels came together
Before the heights of air were raised up
Before the spaces of the sky were named
Before the footstool of the Mountain was established
Before the present years were reckoned up
Before the evil planners were denounced
& those who gather in the jewels of faith were sealed –
Then I considered all of this & through me
& through no other all came into being –
So the end will come through me & through no other

(Hebrew, c. 3rd century A.D.)

From THE GREATER HEKHALOT   "A Cosmic Hymn"

A measure of holiness   a measure of power
A measure of fearfulness   a measure of terror
A measure of trembling   a measure of shaking
A measure of awe   a measure of consternation
Is the measure of the Garment of Zohorariel YaHVeH God of Israel
Who comes crowned in the throne of his own massiveness
& the robe engraved in every part within without is YaHVeH
    YaHVeH
& no creature that has eyes to look at it
Not the eyes of flesh & blood the eyes of many servants
& whoever looks upon it sees or glimpses it
Whirling gyrations grip his eyeballs
Eyeballs as his eyes flash cast out torches
& enkindle him & burn him
For the fire that emerges from the man who looks
Enkindles him & burns him
Why?
Because it is the garment of Zohorariel YaHVeH God of Israel
Who comes crowned to the throne of his own massiveness

J.R. / H.L.

COMMENTARY

(1) Toward the *Ein-Sof,* the "endless," "limitless," or this: the basic proposition
of the search: for what is out of reach, unknowable: the secret of the Jewish
mysteries that strains the powers of a language. Here the poetry is in the telling, *is*
the telling: the account through language, by whatever means, to approach the
secret by its outer forms: as rays, as emanations, as bodies, as images, as sounds, as
words, as names. But the process thus stated is doomed to fail, for the *Ein-Sof,*
writes Gershom Scholem (*Kabbalah,* page 89), is "not accessible even to the in-
nermost thought of the contemplative," rather "a term or image signifying the
domain of the hidden God that lies beyond any impulse toward creation." As one
instance this leads to that (gnostic) dualism in which our world becomes, exists, in
separation as the creation of a second force completely evil. Otherwise, as here, the
limitless ("beyond all thought") is that to which all thought somehow returns as
source. "Cause of all causes." Or again: "Root of all roots."

(2) Rabbi Simeon cited the following from the Book of Mystery. "The Divine Name has both a revealed & an undisclosed form. In its revealed form it is written Y-H-V-H, but in its undisclosed form it is written in other letters, this undisclosed form representing the most Recondite of all." (*Zohar:* Numbers 146b.)

(3) *Hekhalot* = Palaces or Halls, referring to the Divine Throne, etc. For more on this, see throughout "A Book of Powers."

Edmond Jabès (French, b. 1912)
From ELYA

Door II
(THE NAME)

With your screams you have composed his name. And every scream is one of the letters which names you.

To learn my name from the sign. To spell and fear, to cherish and flee it.

To learn reading my life in the Book of the Dead.
Anguish glows above the ashes.
On the log the flame takes its revenge against the forest.
To reach the sky where the fire spreads.
Day recovers its unity.
Morning by
morning,
night by
night.
      . . . .

ROSMARIE WALDROP

Moses de Leon (Aramaic, c. 1240–1305)

From THE GREAT HOLY ASSEMBLY   "The Names"

(First Set)

(1) In my distress I called upon the Lord
(2) The Lord answered me with generosity
(3) The Lord is with me. I shall not fear
(4) The Lord is with me among those who help me
(5) It is better to trust in the Lord
(6) It is better to trust in the Lord

(Second Set)

(1) The Lord is with me. I shall not fear: what can Adam do to me
(2) It is better to trust in the Lord than to trust in Adam
(3) It is better to trust in the Lord than to trust in princes

(Third Set)

(1) In my distress I called upon the Lord
(2) The Lord answered me with generosity
(3) The Lord is with me. I shall not fear
(4) What can Adam do to me
(5) The Lord is with me among those who help me
(6) I will gaze upon those who despise me
(7) It is better to trust in the Lord
(8) Than to trust in Adam
(9) It is better to trust in the Lord than to trust in princes

(*Zohar*)

ROY A. ROSENBERG

COMMENTARY

(1) Naming as a primal language happening, later transferred to the written word as well. Writes Gershom Scholem: "Revelation is revelation of the name or names of God, which are perhaps the different modes of His active being. God's language has no grammar; it consists only of names." And Joseph Gikatilla (14th century): "The whole Torah is nothing but the great name of God."

(2) The "names" above as verses from tradition reassembled (in this case Psalm 118.5 – .9): a process like African praise-namings, etc. Here the verses are taken as the celebration (by David as orphic poet) of the "nine formations of the Divine Beard," itself a sacred "name" of God. The third set is a reassembling of the first two.

The namings below proceed by "lights" & other means.

(Hebrew, c. 17th century)

From SEFER RAZIEL   "Hymn"

He promises His Name. They praise its power and beauty.
He promises through the treasures of snow.
They praise in flux of fire,
In lustrum clouds and flashing palaces.
He who rides the sky promises,
And their praise sweeps through the armies.
He promises the Mystery of the Flame.
They praise through voices of thunder
And quick flashing lightning.
Earth praises, abyss praises,
Waves of the seas praise.
Praise the pristine Name on the throne in each soul
In each creature
Infinitely.

JACK HIRSCHMAN

Naftali Bacharach (Hebrew, 17th century)

A Poem for the Sefirot As a Wheel of Light

(THE IMAGE)

. . . .

(THE RIM)

& going 'round
the ten
sefirot
of
the ball
& orbit
of the world
of first space

. . . .

(THE SPOKES)

1
crown

light from light
extreme light

2
wisdom

splendor from splendor
hidden light

3
understanding

sparkle from sparkle
sparking light

4
greatness

splendor from splendor
pure light

5
power

light from splendor
of light   pure

6
beauty

sparkle from light
light shining

7
victory

light from sparkle
light refined

8
majesty

splendor from sparkle
light bright

9
foundation

sparkle from splendor
purer light
pure   pure

10
kingdom

most precious precious
shining light is

J.R. / H.L.

COMMENTARY

(1) Medieval Jewish *poesis* plays off the image of ten *sefirot* (emanations) as the resonance of *Ein-Sof* (the limitless) into the world of our possible perception. Unified within God – goes one telling – or identical with him, they appear to the human mind as differentiated stages, mapped in a sacred language game by words descriptive of their source. Thus from the First Book of Chronicles (29.11) come the terms *gedula* (greatness), *gevura* (power), *tiferet* (beauty), *netsah* (victory), *hod* (majesty), & *malkhut* (kingdom), to which are added the three upper *sefirot*: *keter* (crown), *hokhma* (wisdom), & *bina* (understanding), in the most common of the sefirotic namings. Synonyms for *sefirot* do in fact include *shemot*, names, & *diburim*, sayings, but they are also known as lights, powers, crowns, qualities, garments, mirrors, shoots, sources, sapphires, & their configuration imaged as a tree, a man, a chariot, a series of concentric circles or reflected lights, even (thus Scholem): "a

candle flickering in the midst of ten mirrors set one within the other, each a different color." (For an earlier formulation in which the *sefirot* = letters & numbers, see page 62, below.)

In the present instance the "wheel of light" is not a fixed or static image (from which the "limitless" could as well be excluded) but an image in motion & tied finally to the mystery of creation as worked through by the 16th-century kabbalist & poet Isaac Luria. Here the limitless that fills all space contracts itself to leave a point or vacuum behind in which the universe originates. The act of withdrawal is called *tsimtsum* ("contraction") & the point is called *tehiru*, the primordial space. A ray of light moving across this circular space fills it with the ten *sefirot*, which surround it like a wheel of light. Only a residue of *Ein-Sof* stays within it – like little drops of oil.

(2) "At the outset the decision of the King made a tracing in the supernal effulgence, a lamp of scintillation, & there issued within the impenetrable recesses of the mysterious limitless a shapeless nucleus enclosed in a ring, neither white nor black nor red nor green nor any color at all. . . . The most mysterious Power enshrouded in the limitless then split, without splitting its void, remaining wholly unknowable until from the force of the strokes there shone forth a supernal & mysterious point. Beyond that point there is no knowable, & therefore it is called *Reshit* (beginning), the creative utterance which is the starting-point of all." (*Zohar:* Genesis 15a.)

(3) "One can disintegrate the world by means of very strong light. For weak eyes the world becomes solid, for still weaker eyes it seems to develop fists, for eyes weaker still it becomes shamefaced and smashes anyone who dares to gaze upon it." (Franz Kafka, *Reflections on Sin, Suffering, Hope & the True Way.*)

Jackson Mac Low (b. 1922)

1ST LIGHT POEM: FOR IRIS – 10 JUNE 1962

The light of a student-lamp
sapphire light
shimmer
the light of a smoking-lamp

Light from the Magellanic Clouds
the light of a Nernst lamp
the light of a naphtha-lamp
light from meteorites

Evanescent light
ether
the light of an electric lamp
extra light

Citrine light
kineographic light
the light of a Kitson lamp
kindly light

Ice light
irradiation
ignition
altar light

The light of a spotlight
a sunbeam
sunrise
solar light

Mustard-oil light
Maroon light
the light of a magnesium flare
light from a meteor

Evanescent light
ether
light from an electric lamp
an extra light

Light from a student-lamp
sapphire light
a shimmer
smoking-lamp light

Ordinary light
orgone lumination
light from a lamp burning olive oil
opal light

Actinism
atom-bomb light
the light of an alcohol lamp
the light of a lamp burning anda-oil

Ishmael ben Elisha (Hebrew, c. 2nd century A.D.)

From SHI'UR KOMA   "The Measure of the Body"

This is the measure of the stature spoken in the Book of the Measure

"Great is our lord *and much power*"

236,000 leagues   the height of the Creator be He blessed   The measure
of his league is 3 miles   and the mile is 10,000 cubits   and the cubit is 3
spans   and the span fills the whole world   and there is another account-
ing besides this   a thousand thousand myriad myriad and six-hundred
thousand myriad and nine thousand myriad and sixty-two myriad   thirty-
nine hundred leagues and thirteen leagues and a third of a league   and
Rabbi Ishmael ben Elisha the high priest noted that the measure in all is

two thousand myriad leagues of a myriad myriads   one thousand leagues high   one thousand thousand myriad leagues broad   The measure of his league is three miles   and the mile is ten thousand cubits   and the cubit is three spans   and the span fills the whole world   as it is said   "The skies with a span you set up"

So much according to Rabbi Ishmael

H.L.

COMMENTARY

(1) For all its highly touted image-breaking tendencies – from Abraham's iconoclasting the Chaldean statues onward – the Jewish enterprise develops a range of phanopoeia (image-making) as fantastic as any going in the ancient Near East. Such traditions, usually called esoteric, may better be viewed as the surfacing, or the maintenance as hidden oral lore (kabbala), of those other, by then sub-terranean, cultures against which the makers of the Torah wrote: "You shall de-stroy their images & cut down their groves," etc. (Exodus 34.13.) As a still accept-able *ma'ase merkaba* (i.e., "the work of the chariot" – after the vision in the first chapter of Ezekiel) it proliferated into attempts to "see" & "measure" the chariot, the throne, the wheels, the living creatures, the image of the man-god on the throne, the halls, the doors, the palaces of heaven. The other great image-making areas of that time were apocalypse (visualizations, that is, of the end of our known world) & the so-called "work of creation": & these, along with talmudic exegeses, ritual & moral reinterpretations of the Bible, Hellenistic commentaries, poems & incantations, produced a work of such dimensions that the historian Michael Grant can conclude that Jewish *poesis* not only didn't end with the final transcriptions of the Bible but that "the Jews, almost uniquely among the subjects of Rome, had pro-duced and were still producing an extensive literature of their own."

(2) *Shi'ur Koma,* or "measure of the body," is the culmination of the shaman-like journey of the merkaba mystic through heavens & cosmic palaces & into the pres-ence of the "image of the man-god on the chair." From measurement of the height, the description goes on to various parts of the body, measuring & naming them. The version here is attributed to Ishmael ben Elisha, 2nd-century contemporary & companion of Rabbi Akiba. The procedure begins numerologically, by adding up the letters (numbers) in Psalm 147.5 "& much power" (*ve-rav koah*) = 236, then multiplying by 1,000 leagues, etc.

(Hebrew/Aramaic, medieval)

FOR THE BEARD OF THE GREAT FACE
"A Vision & Poem"

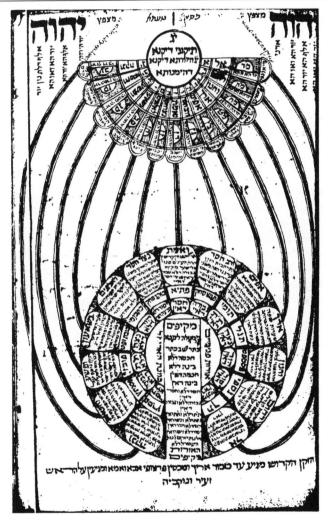

GLOSS: The two lines at the bottom read: *The Holy Beard goes as far as the navel of the Great Face & covers the faces of the Father & the Mother & rests upon the head of the Small Face & the Female.*

COMMENTARY

(1) Naming becomes the speaking of a vision, in which speech & sight, language & vision, are in constant interplay. The word creates the vision, vision images the word – as language by outracing sight asserts a paradox & puts a face (or, rather, *faces*) on [H.L.: makes faces at] the limitless. And even for the Jews, as martyrs (witnesses) to the "One God," the mind mirrors an infinite series of such images. More characteristically the reduction is to three or four – as here, the Great Face, Small Face, & Shekinah, the Father, the Son, & the Mother/the Bride, who are also the trinity of the early Jewish Christians; elsewhere a quaternity, in which the sacred name, the tetragrammaton, is read as Y the Father, H the Mother, V the Son, & H the Daughter, sometimes taken as a pair of androgynous figures. Thus, Raphael Patai's translation of a key passage from the *Zohar:* "The Supernal H (i.e. the Mother) became pregnant as a result of all the love and fondling – since the Y never leaves her – and she brought forth the V (the Son), whereupon she stood up and suckled him. And when the V emerged, his female mate (the Daughter, represented by the second H in the Tetragrammaton) emerged together with him." (*The Hebrew Goddess,* page 174.)

(2) As an extension of the *Shi'ur Koma* impulse (see above), the later Jewish image-making extends to the appearance of the Great Face and the Small Face – most complexly to their "beards." The Beard of the Great Face appears in thirteen configurations or segments describing "mercy," that of the Small Face in nine describing "power" – of which much else is said in "The Book of Conceal-ment," "The Great Holy Assembly," & "The Lesser Holy Assembly" of the *Zohar.*

The visualization, above, maps out the thirteen measures of mercy in the Ancient One's beard. "The beard" is itself taken as another name of God.

(3) "All faces are His. Hence, He has no face. – Reb Alen" (From E. Jabès, *The Book of Questions.*)

Isaac Luria (Aramaic, 1534–72)

A POEM FOR THE SMALL FACE

sons of his palace
were shy
who witness rays from
the small face

these to be here
at this table
the king cuts
grooves from his ring in

be pleased with
this meeting
this center of powers
all wingd

to bring joy to it
now
is his hour of peace
without anger

draw near me
thou see my companions
be night without
judgment

those dogs
wild with *chutzpah*
keep out
may not enter

but send for
Ancient of Days
exchanging
the jewel in his forehead

his peace
as he sees it
releases the light from
the shells

& will flow with it
into each orifice
these will conceal
under domes

will be here
in praise of the evening
a poem for
the small face

J.R.

COMMENTARY

The Small Face is the "son" of the tetragrammaton (YHVH), who as the reflection, even the inversion, of the Ancient of Days, is known as the "impatient one" (= *ze'ir anpin* = "small face"), the angry face of the reality confronting us. Anyone who opens to suffering – who, like the schizophrenic, leaves his nerve endings raw, unguarded – will recognize that face as "evil," not in a moralizing sense but as part of a science (poetics would be a better term) of contraries, kept alive by poets & other visionaries in an age of literalized "belief." Viewed otherwise, as "the godhead in its endless growth & development" (G. Scholem), the Small Face is the bridegroom of the Shekinah, & their marriage is celebrated at the Sabbath. Like the gods of the earlier fertility religions, he is heaven & she is earth; or drawing from the going Jewish god-names, he is Yahveh & she is Elohim.

The "shells" (*klipot*) of the poem's ending (for which, see below, page 58) are the hard husks, the material, of our world, covering over those seeds or germs of light that are the remnants of *Ein-Sof*'s withdrawal in the act of *tsimtsum* (see above, page 25). In meditation, etc., participants worked with the Ancient of Days & the Small Face to release the light toward that "cleansing of the doors of perception" that William Blake named for us in his recovery & invention of an actual poetics. Then would come the sensual awakening & the inflow of light through the body's orifices: the union of God & his bride.

The occasion of Luria's "Poem for the Small Face" was the Sabbath celebration by his circle of mystics in the city of Safed. It marked the final meal of the Sabbath, as the "Poem for the Shekinah" that follows marked the opening, & its intent was to drive off distractions by the unreconstructed forces of "the other side," to allow a balance of powers within the world itself. Writes Scholem: "It is not a mere description of an exorcism, it *is* an exorcism." (*On the Kabbalah and Its Symbolism*, page 145.)

Isaac Luria (Aramaic, 1534–72)

A POEM FOR THE SHEKINAH
ON THE FEAST OF THE SABBATH

I have sung
an old measure

would open
gates to

her field of apples
(each one a power)

set a new table
to feed her

& beautifully
candelabrum

drops its
light on us

Between right & left
the Bride

draws near in
holy jewels

clothes of the sabbath
whose lover

embraces her
down to foundation

gives pleasure
squeezes his strength out

in surcease of
sorrow

& makes new faces
be hers

& new souls
new breath

gives her joy
double measure

of lights & of
streams for her blessing

o Friends of the Bride
go forth

all's sealed
within her

shines out from
Ancient of Days

Toward the south
I placed

candelabrum
(o mystical)

room in
the north

for table
for bread

for pitchers of wine
for sweet myrtle

gives power to
lovers

new potencies
garlands

give her many
sweet foods to taste

many kinds of
fish

for fertility
birth

of new souls
new spirits

will follow the 32 paths
& 3 branches

the bride with
70 crowns

with her King who
hovers above her

crown above crown in
Holy of Holies

this lady all worlds are
formed in

of words for her
70 crowns

50 gates
the Shekinah

ringed by
6 loaves

of the sabbath
& bound

all sides to
Heavenly Refuge

the hostile
powers

have left us
demons you feared

sleep in chains

J.R.

COMMENTARY

(1) "*Shekhina* is the frequently used Talmudic term denoting the visible and audible manifestation of God's presence on earth. In its ultimate development as it appears in the late Midrash literature, the Shekhina concept stood for an independent, feminine divine entity prompted by her compassionate nature to argue with God in defense of man. She is thus, if not by character, then by function and position, a direct heir to such ancient Hebrew goddesses of Canaanite origin as Asherah and Anath." (Raphael Patai, *The Hebrew Goddess,* page 137.) She is identified with the tenth *sefira – Malkhut,* or Kingdom – & her counterpart among the *sefirot* of the left side is Lilith, "the night wailer." Her reappearance among us is an event of contemporary *poesis, not* religion – "She / in whom the Jew has his communion / . . . maiden to the eye." (Robert Duncan.)

(2) "In the usage of the Kabbalah . . . the Shekhinah becomes an aspect of God, a quasi-independent feminine element within Him. . . . [The conception of] the exile of the Shekhinah goes back to the Talmud, 'In every exile into which the children of Israel went, the Shekhinah was with them.' In the Talmud this means only that God's presence was always with Israel in its exiles. In the Kabbalah, however, it is taken to mean that a part of God Himself is exiled from God. . . . The exile of Shekhinah . . . in other words . . . [is] the separation of the masculine and feminine principles in God." (G. Scholem, *On the Kabbalah & Its Symbolism,* 1965.)

(Hebrew, c. 3rd century A.D.)

From THE GREATER HEKHALOT   "The Door Keepers"

the 7th palace
standing at the gate
    & angry
           war like
   strong
harsh
         fearful
   furious
the height of mountains
brightness of the peaks
with bows strung stood before them
sharpened swords in hands
the play of lightnings out of eye balls
balls of fire from their nostrils
torches coals from mouths
wore helmets crowns
& iron coats
         spears
    javelins
width of their arms
these keepers of the gates
o these with horses
   they would ride now stand
   side of the stables troughs of fire
   coals of juniper
   they eat o fire of the mangers
   drops like 40 bushels in one mouthful
   horses mouths each mouth
   3 stables of Caesarea
   each stable was the width of
   Caesar's Gate
& rivers also fire ran beside
the stables horses drank from

like fullness of the water works
in Kidron
cistern that contains
the rain that ever fell
down all Jerusalem

J.R.

COMMENTARY

(1) The visionary journey, first called an "ascent" but not long after "going down" or "in": "descent *into* the chariot" that gave its name (*merkaba* = "chariot" = "metaphor" by punning) to the process: therefore a trip into the mind of the initiate himself. And if we now think of all that as *poesis*, as an ongoing creation through those techniques that Eliade tells us were the great resources of the early shaman-poets ("technicians of the sacred"), the link to the subterranean tradition is here all the clearer. The ecstasy & the journey do persist, then, & the impulse to *poesis* survives the disappearance of the shamans.

What is seen gives a name to the process of seeing & speaking: as *ma'ase merkaba* ("work of the chariot," defined above) or as *hekhalot* (books of palaces & halls encountered on the trip), in the vocabulary of mystics from the first & second centuries. But while the journey was possible in other directions (even to the anti-worlds, of contraries, destructive of our own), it is the sky-trip that was the most illuminated, as if even the first shaman-poets, the ones at source, were specialists in the "descent to heaven" – like the Altai shamans climbing to the sky, to see the great god Ulgan on his throne, surrounded by guards & mystic animals, much like the *hayot* ("living creatures") in the prophetic visions of Ezekiel & onward. The record that results is at once fantastic architecture & cosmology, a series of maps & blueprints, marked with threats & dangers, even – the more occulted & doubtful the tradition becomes (thus: Kafka's parable, "Before the Law") – with presentiments of the trip deferred.

(2) from "the notebooks"   9/75   not hell's brilliance   butterflies that sting   stung us into vision   but as here   illumination of the mind   is from the upper worlds   their hell mere ugliness   so that the pain of vision terror   finds its place in heaven   though it blinds the eye

. . . .

(variation)

& I never knew heaven could be terrible as hell   or be as bright   (j.r.)

Tristan Tzara (French, 1896–1963)

ANGEL

color recomposes
the liquid hanged men
worms of light in the vapor
where the clarinets grow
the bell glides under the boat
below the town flame bandages
squeeze squeeze tightly
the feldspar gleams in the speed
on holiday
mechanic of necrologies
staging of the menageries
then throws at her husband's head

meeeeeteeeeooooroooolooo-
giies
the sun glides tangent of the atmo-
sphere
skating dimensions

flows between the spaces
rainbow swing
where our durations are visible
woman pregnant with satellites
burning green ball
caress the centrifugal wound
bellies' acids and plant
angel mechanic
windmill
negro head
and of friendships
a bowl of vitriol
let's go to the other
meterologies

glide aureola

PIERRE JORIS

COMMENTARY

(1) "From every utterance that goes forth from the mouth of the Holy One Be Blest an angel is created, as they say: *By the word of Yahveh were the heavens made, & all the host of them by the breath of Yahveh's mouth*." (Talmud: Ḥagiga 14a.)

(2) And Rilke: "Every single angel is terrible. . . . " Or again: "This 'angel' . . . has nothing to do with the Angel of the Christian heaven (rather with the angelic figures of Islam) . . . in whom the transformation of the visible into the invisible we are performing already appears complete . . . therefore 'terrible' to us, because we, its lovers and transformers, still depend on the visible." Thus: "The world, regarded no longer from the human point of view, but as it is within the angel, is perhaps my real task, one, at any rate, in which all my previous attempts would converge." (1925, 1915.)

(3) "Said Rabbi Simeon: Alas for the blindness of the sons of men, all unaware as they are how full the earth is of strange & invisible beings & hidden dangers, which could they but see, they would marvel how they themselves can exist on the earth." (*Zohar* 1.55a.)

Moses of Burgos (Hebrew, 1230/1235–c. 1300)

From THE BOOK OF THE LEFT PILLAR

> ... *& he set up the pillars in the porch of the temple   he set up the right pillar & named it Jachin & set up the left pillar & named it Boaz ...* (I KINGS 7.21.)

as the idea arose in the mind of God & in his pure thought to create a holy & a pure reality, the foundation & the pillar of perfection, to let all good things pour forth from his majesty ... so the idea arose in his divine & pure will to create real beings according to an order & arrangement too diverse, too darkly wonderful, too distant & too strange for its logical comprehension by any of the masters of rational knowledge & of exegesis   :   but there is a reliable tradition, a kabbala passed on to all the masters of the hidden wisdom, that reality as a whole could not exist except through real beings, beings that do good & that do evil, that bring things into being & sustain them, that terminate & that obliterate, that give rewards & punishments   : & THE ELOHIM HAS DONE THIS SO THAT MEN SHOULD FEAR BEFORE HIM (Ecclesiastes 3.14) as Solomon has said THE ONE AS WELL AS THE OTHER ELOHIM HAS MADE (Ecclesiastes 7.14)   :   & our wise ones, may their memory be a blessing, said: HE CREATED THE RIGHTEOUS, HE CREATED THE WICKED, HE CREATED PARADISE, HE CREATED HELL, TO SHOW THAT HE CREATED ALL THINGS & THEIR OPPOSITIONS (Talmud: *Ḥagiga* 15a)   : & the Prophet said I FORM THE LIGHT & CREATE DARKNESS, I MAKE PEACE & CREATE EVIL, I YAHVEH DO ALL THESE THINGS (Isaiah 45.7)   :   & listen   :   from the meaning of these verses we can understand & we can know that He, the Holy One Be Blest, made all things & also made their contraries, & perfectly he did his perfect work perfecting his perfection for the good ones, those whose hearts are straight   :   & he created evil   :   a new reality of being appointed to bring suffering & punishments on rebels & on sinners & on all who walk the dark & gloomy road   :   the unpaved way

J.R. / H.L.

COMMENTARY

(1) "Without Contraries is no progression. Attraction and Repulsion, Reason and Energy, Love and Hate, are necessary to Human existence.

"From these contraries spring what the religious call Good & Evil. Good is the passive that obeys Reason. Evil is the active springing from Energy.

"Good is Heaven. Evil is Hell."

(Thus Wm. Blake, "The Marriage of Heaven & Hell," circa 1790.)

(2) With Moses of Burgos, etc., we are straining the limits of the "normative," non-dualistic religion. But the move occurs again & again, even erupts (with Jewish gnostics & inspired heretics, say) into the idea of a true counter-force: the "powers" of the world we know as the essential contraries of *Ein-Sof*, etc. And it is that split in turn that lays the groundwork for a virtual "poetics of liberation."

While such a formulation tends as here to remain a moral metaphor, it can be read more interestingly as a dialectic & a "metapoetics" (G. Quasha): a complex imagery of worlds & counter-worlds. Thus the world of the "right side" is matched point for point by a world of the "other side" (the so-called *sitra aḥra*) or left side, left hand, or left pillar – spinning like anti-matter in the opposite direction. Moses of Burgos even supplies names for the counter-*sefirot* (see above), although the designations seem more spooky than substantive, viz: THE 10 SEFIROT OF THE LEFT ACCORDING TO MOSES OF BURGOS: (1) Tomi'el or Twin El (maybe: twin of Keter), or Tumi'el: Complete El; (2) 'Ugi'el: Encircled El, or Go'iy'el: the Bleating El; (3) Sitri'el: the Secret El, or Harasi'el: Destroyed El; (4) Ga'ashkala: Shaking to the End; (5) Geyvlahav: Backfire; (6) Tagiriron: the Challenge; (7) 'Arav Tsarak: maybe Spurned the Sweets (wrote Rambam) as "God's Sweetness"; (8) Sama'el: Defiant Rebel, or Sama'el: Gives Death; (9) Gamali'el: the Weaning Camel, or Naḥashi'el: Snake El, or camel with its legs cut off; & (10) Lilith: the Night Wailer (match her up with Malkhut as a female presence): the Shekinah of the Left.

David Meltzer (b. 1937)

From HERO / LIL   "The Third Shell"

---

*And behold, that hard shell (i.e. embodiment of evil), Lilith, is always present in
the bedlinen of man and wife when they copulate, in order to take hold of the sparks
of the drops of semen which are lost – because it is impossible to perform the marital
act without such a loss of sparks – and she creates out of them demons, spirits and
Lilin. . . . But there is an incantation for this, to chase Lilith away from the bed
and to bring forth pure souls . . . in that moment, when a man copulates with his
wife, let him direct his heart to the holiness of his Master, and say;*

> *"In the name of God.*
> *O you who are wrapped in velvet*
> *You have appeared.*
> *Release, release!*
> *Neither come nor go!*
> *The seed is not yours,*
> *Nor in your inheritance.*
> *Go back, go back!*
> *The sea rages,*
> *Its waves call you.*
> *I hold on to the Holy One,*
> *Wrap myself into the King's holiness."*

> From: *Emek Ha-Melekh*
> (*Sha'ar Tikkune Ha-teshuvah*)

(1)

L	Y	L	Y	T
30	10	30	10	400

*

30 10 30 10 400 = 480 = 12

*

The book within the book.
All year long. Night & day.

(2)

The embrace.
Locked in love.
Man inside woman,
Woman inside man.
Yod in Hay,
Hay in Yod.
The halves made whole.

(3)

Lilith: process.
One end of the imagination to the other.
Start & stop in her core.
Fill her bowl with light.
She is song.
Song goes thru
Seed in her womb.
Her womb is Aleph.
First woman. Before Eve.
Last woman.
Matronita, Shekinah.
Brides of God.
Within me.
The process.

(4)

Into the Hay of her, the Hay within the Hay within the Hay of her,
as thru door after door of her. All combinations of her interchange. Face
into face. Sex into sex. All sparks & specks sing a multitude of possibility.
Into the Hay of her, the Hay within the Hay within the Hay of her.

Her grace made more so by completion

Upper & lower cherubic spheres extend & pipeline light thru all
our veins. Birth the triumph, creation the song of it.

Flesh vanity. A shell our eyes touch & appraise. Skin deep.

Before & after each pass, praise her invisible tongue.

(5)

"To banish his loneliness, Lilith was first given to Adam as wife. Like him she had been created from the dust of the ground. But she remained with Adam only a short time, because she insisted upon enjoying full equality with her husband. She derived her right from their identical origin."

From: *Midrash Bereshit Rabbah.*

(6)

Words thrown back.
Stars, suns, moons.
We fear her more than He.
His thunder speech
Can not hide the need for union.
We father daughters to reach her.
Words thrown back.
Man stands at root end
Pointing to her door.
Words thrown back.
Stones against her window.
Jewels thrown at her feet.
Stars, suns, moon.
Letters snow upon her gold crown as she walks by.

(7)

At night I touch her mouth with language. Afterwards. I move against her. She spends all day dressing for night, preparing her face. I am a farmer. She asks me to light her pipe. We are married by flashlight. She stands in a circle of raccoons. I drive a machine of letters. We are behind the wheel. The radio's on. She caresses my shoulder blades. A field of corn turns into mercury sheets her body swims under. Law is reversed at night, black is white & white black. She wants words only after sunrise. I touch her mouth with language. Afterwards. I move against her.

(8)

> "You have made a mistake."
> "Try the other door. It's really locked."
> "You only think it's God."
> "Your name has been reversed."
> "No tricks."
> "Don't ever get used to being cheated."
> "It still hasn't been said. Give her another kiss."
> "No book should be longer."

(9)

> "Her radiance, however, is so great that the angels must cover their faces with their wings so as not to see her. The ministering angels are removed from the Shekinah by myriads of parasangs, and the body of Shekinah herself measures millions of miles."
>
> From: *Midrash Ha-Gadol Shemini*.

(10)

> Ah you old whore
> step halfway out the blue door
> with Woolworth mirror bangles
> & burlesque spangles
> & wink at any guy
> passing by
> minding his own
> business.
>
> We all know Lilith
> as she moves

COMMENTARY

"No she-demon has ever achieved as fantastic a career as Lilith who started out from the lowliest of origins, was a failure as Adam's intended wife, became the paramour of lascivious spirits, rose to be the bride of Samael the demon king, ruled as the Queen of Zemargad and Sheba, and finally ended up as the consort of God himself." (Raphael Patai, *The Hebrew Goddess*, page 207.)

108. And God warned Israel. He said, "If you will attend to the voice of God . . . " This may be compared to a king, who had a beautiful daughter and others desired her. The king heard of the matter and, since he could not strive against those who were trying to lead his daughter into evil conduct he warned his daughter, "Do not attend the words of these who would harm you and they will not overcome you. Do not go to the opening of the house. Do your work inside; never be idle; and they can never see you nor do you harm. For they have a certain Character: they keep distant from every good way and choose every evil way. And when they see someone directing himself along a good way and walking upon it they hate him."

109. And who is this? The satan. This gives instruction that God has a Character and its name is "Evil." And it is in the north as it is written, "The evil shall open forth from the north." That is, any evil which comes to any of the dwellers of the earth comes from the north.

And what is this Character? It is the form of a hand. It has many emissaries and the name of them all is "evil, evil," though there are greater and lesser among them. They destroy the world; for Tohu is to the north and Tohu means nothing other than that which confuses man until it causes him to sin. It is the origin of all the evil nature in man.

And why is it set to the left? Because it has no domain in the world but in the north. It seeks only to be in the north and is only used to the north. Since if it were to be in the south until it learned the ways of the south then how could it pervert man? It would be hindered those days it was learning and not be able to cause man to sin. Therefore it is always to the left and this is what is meant by what is written, "The nature of man's heart is evil from his youth." It is evil since its youth and turned only towards the left for there it is already used to be. Thus it is that God said to Israel, "If you will attend to the voice of God and do what is straight in his eyes and give ear to his commandments" – and not to the commandments of the evil nature – "and keep his laws" – and not the law of the evil nature – "I, God, am your healer."

H.L.

COMMENTARY

Sefer ha-Bahir ("The Book of Brightness") – viewed as the earliest work of kabbalistic literature as such – first appeared in 12th-century Provence, with intimations of connections into even deeper sources. A short, loosely structured midrash or assemblage of statements attributed to a string of sometimes fictive rabbis, it reads, in David Meltzer's good description, like "a collage of voices on the page, which appear and disappear like the mysterious rabbis in Edmond Jabès's *Book of Questions.* . . . Intangible and ineffable fragments from a lost book."

CODA

Yosef ibn Abitur (Hebrew, mid-10th century – c. 1012)
THE "WHO?" OF IBN ABITUR OF CORDOBA

who
ANCHORED the high skies
set off the wheels for those who shine
who'd
BE a god as great as El
could tell El's greatness
who
COMES to praise El Elohim
with silence
who
DID speak & speech became
the day he pitched his skies
who
EMITTED utterance & utterance remained
the day he set his earths

who
     FIXED the ocean's depth
          the day he placed his lines
who
     GLUED earth's clods together
          the day he laid his valleys' floors
who
     HELD its measurements in place
          whose plumbline touched the earth
who's
     IN a king's robe
          fancy garments
who
     JUDGES righteousness
          on country roads
who's
     KNOWN as strong Yah many-powered
          all who stand up bow to him
who
     LETS out secrets drop by drop
          then names them speaking
who
     MAKES speech bring to life without his word
          but him
who
     NARROWED the sea breakers
          into sea deeps
who
     OPENED 300 horses' hoofs
          between each wave
who
     PRONOUNCED words
          that broke a channel for the current
who
     QUESTIONED the rain coming
          two drops at a time to wash it out
who
     ROUNDED up the winds in his cupped palm
          trapped the waters in his robe

who
> SIGNALS ninety-nine
>> birthshrieks for the mountain goat

who
> TOLD the eagle she could grasp her children
>> in between her wings ascending

who
> URGED the dragon
>> to bite the goat's womb

who
> VISIONS to every thunderclap
>> a roadway of its own

who
> BROKE a channel for the current
>> a road for his bolts of lightning

who
> YIELDED to every man
>> the number of hairs for his head

who
> YET made each hair unique
>> to keep from jamming together

who
> ORNAMENTED what man constructs
>> like the beauty of first-born Adam

who
> SAID that this should be like that
>> same form same speech same voice

who
> EXPRESSES commands to his face
>> & pays him when he obeys

whose
> FIVE fears were instilled
>> in the five great beasts of this world

who
> ORDAINED a fear of mosquitoes
>> beneath the elephant's thick hide

who
> FORCED the fear of the squirmer
>> on ancient Leviathan

who
    CALLED out loud to show them
        that he rules over them all
who
    OPPOSES his ways
        & can soften his heart to peace
who
    REVERSES oppressed & oppressor
        so oppressor can't break loose
who
    DREW the sudden fear of the locust
        over the lion's mind
who
    OVERCOMES the scorpion
        with fear of the squirming spider
who
    BROUGHT the fear of the swallow
        to the eagle up in the sky
who
    ANCHORED the ends of the earth

J.R. / H.L.

THE END OF "A BOOK OF POWERS"

A Book of Worlds

(beginning)   these are the generations of the skies & earth   when they were created   the day when Yahveh Elohim made earth & skies.

(Genesis 2.4.)

Joseph Gikatilla (Hebrew, 1248–c. 1325)

THE WITHDRAWAL, THE EXILE

The semicircular line of print reads: *a dot the nations of the world surround the circle are outside & Israel's the middle of the dot.*

COMMENTARY

(1) The image of *tsimtsum* (see above, page 24) is the world defined by God's withdrawal. Pinpoint at center of the circle. Empty space. With creation, emergence, it enters history, exists now in the consciousness that grows around it. The world we know begins: a world of growth, division into shapes & species: builds toward the myth of exile: Jewish, gnostic. But the point is there for each of us, renewed at each conception, flashes up, ovum ignited, swelling, screaming our entry into light. This is birth: creation felt by the created. Surrounded, absent in ourselves, each one the dot, the focal point, the center. Each one of us is now called Israel, now fills the place of exile with our absent god.

(2) In Gikatilla's visualization the third line toward the center is the single word (נקודה) NKVDH = point or dot, while the top line is the god-name (אהוי) AHVY, spelled out as Alef-Hey-Vav-Yod.

Nachman of Bratzlav (Hebrew, 1772 – 1810)
From THE TORAH OF THE VOID

God,
for Mercy's sake,
created the world
to reveal Mercy.
If there were no world
on whom would Mercy take pity?

So – to show His Mercy
He created the worlds
from *Aziluth*'s peak
to this Earth's center.

But as He wished to create
there was not a *where?*
All was Infinitely He,
Be He Blessed!

The light He condensed
sideways
thus was *space* made
an empty void.

In *space* days and measures
came into being.
So the world was created.

This void was needed
for the world's sake,
so that it may be
put into place.

Don't strain to understand
this void!
It is a mystery – not to be realized
until the future
is the *now*.

                    *

Once there was *light*,
much and powerful,
holy *light*,
and it was in vessels
– too much *light*,
too much power –
and the *vessels* burst!

When the *vessels* burst
the fragments
of Holiness
took form
becoming the *outered* sciences.

So,
even of Holiness
there is offal:
Just as there is sweat
and hair and excrement,
so Holiness too
has its offal.

Holy Wisdom too has offal.
Outered wisdom
is the offal of the holy.
And when this offal is used
to twist the world,
you have sorcery.

Once, also, *source-ery*
was rooted
in a high wisdom.

He who can
should strive to avoid
the trap
of the *outered* sciences.
But whoever falls
into the trap
is not lost forever.

Seeking God
one can find Him there,
in the shards of Holiness
which give life to the sciences—
even in the very symbols
in which the sciences
express themselves.
For as long as there
is reason and rhyme—
and words—
there is Holiness
in the form of sparks.
As long as there is life
in the word, God is there.

*

And the void?

It is nothing but
the *no-thing* which takes up
no *space* at all.
All it does is separate

between the Divine which *fills*
and the Divine which *surrounds*
the world.

Without the void
all would have been One.
But then
there would not have been
any creature – any world.
So the void is a kind of
Divine Wisdom of not being
so there can be division
between one kind of being
and another.

This wisdom of not being,
the wisdom of the void –
cannot be realized!
It is not a *something*
but it makes all *somethings* possible.
Each something is infused with
God
and surrounded by God:
There is in between
a void that is not.

                    *

All creation comes from
the WORD:
"By the word of God
Heaven was made,
and by the breath of His mouth
all their hosts."
In words inhere wisdom
and sense.

All speech is bordered
by the five limits
of the mouth.
All creation is a limiting
in three dimensions

and in time
and in substance:
"In wisdom hast Thou
made them all."

The void has no limits,
no echo.
Burning questions
are not answered there.
Martyrs who want to know *Why?*
are told "Silence."
Thus is the decree of the *Thought!*
Such *thought* is not given
to words.

                    *

How is the void made?
By strife!
One *zaddik* says this
and the other that,
and *between*
there is strained a void.

                    *

A *zaddik* sings.
If he is a "Moses"
he can raise souls
lost in the void.

Each science
has its own song:
Each science
issues from a melody.
Even the void's Unwisdom
has a melody of its own.

"What was wrong with the heretic?"
"When he rose,
Greek song books fell from him.
All day he hummed
the Greek's song."

The song and the heresy –
each depends on the other –
the wisdom and its tune,
the science and its scale.
For heresies fall
in bookloads
from one who sings the tune
of heresy.

                *

And through the *zaddik*'s *niggun*,
when in him tonguetied Moses
sings,
all lost souls
rise from the abyss,
find their way from the void.
All tunes are reabsorbed in
the song of silence,
all heresy integrated and dissolved,
Tune and word
in the THOUGHT SONG.

                *

"Moses came to Pharaoh"
– the void –
"and said
Tomorrow –
see –
I bring the *arbeh,*
the swarms
of locusts
into your midst."
For *tomorrow*
is the time
of the reward receiving.

What is the reward all about?
To perceive great perception
to have cosmic insight,
today unattainable.

And then we will know
how the void
was like the locust,
its cloak and being one,
all veils and garments
but He
outer, inner He
word and wordless He
end and endless He
Tune and singer He
Most high and abyss He
void He, fullness He
I-He
You He
He
He!
        —Amen!

ZALMAN SCHACHTER

COMMENTARY

(1) The fullness of "God" described as *ayin,* "nothing" *—for* ayin *combines a thing & its opposite* (thus Abraham Kalisker, circa 1800). This is a further meditation on the image of the "point": the empty (or full) center of the circle: a condensed mass of light or energy about to burst. Yet the idea of the empty center is, however glossed over, a reminder that in a world of contingencies, there are no answers, only questions. Thus Gertrude Stein on her deathbed: "What is the answer?" (Silence.) "Well then, what is the question?"

(2) THE BREAKING OF THE VESSELS. In the vacuum left by God's withdrawal (*tsimtsum*), lines of light pour in, irradiate, collide. Crystal vessels form, which can't contain the light but burst, leaving dark shards behind. The shards (*klipot*) are the basis of all matter & represent the forces of the "other side" (the *sitra aḥra*): the uncleansed "doors of perception" of the familiar world (Wm. Blake). Within them are "sparks" or "seeds" of light, & the intention of the process that follows is the freeing of that light.

    The basic formulation—but more complex & image-filled than that given here—is Isaac Luria's. Like gnosticism—to which it is related—it traces the condition of a broken (i.e., imperfect) universe away from man & back to "source" as "god" or "nothing." The "breaking of the vessels" is also called "the death of the kings."

Joseph Gikatilla (Hebrew, 1248 – c. 1325)

NOTHING

I.

COMMENTARY

(1) In Hebrew: AYIN (אין) / Aniy (אני), an anagram in which the pronoun *aniy* (I) is a name of God, as *ayin* (nothing) is his attribute in *tsimtsum.* On the use of pronouns (I, He, Thou) as names of God, the reader may want to check the *Zohar;* e.g.: "It is written, 'I, the Lord, am the first and with the last: I am He' (Isaiah 41.4). Everything is He: He is the name concealed on all sides." (130a.) Or again: "*And Thou shalt rule over him:* the word 'thou' contains a mystical allusion to the Almighty, who is also called THOU." (1.37a.)

(2) "Men have addressed their eternal *Thou* with many names. In singing of Him who was thus named they always had the *Thou* in mind: the first myths were hymns of praise. Then the names took refuge in the language of *It;* men were more and more strongly moved to think of and to address their eternal *Thou* as an *It.* But all God's names are hallowed, for in them He is not merely spoken about, but also spoken to.

". . . He who speaks the word God and really has *Thou* in mind (whatever the illusion by which he is held), addresses the true *Thou* of his life, which cannot be limited by another *Thou,* and to which he stands in a relation that gathers up and includes all others.

"But when he, too, who abhors the name, and believes himself to be godless, gives his whole being to addressing the *Thou* of his life, as a *Thou* that cannot be limited by another, he addresses God." (Martin Buber, *I and Thou.*)

Franz Kafka (German, 1883 – 1924)

FRAGMENT

"Never will you draw the water out of the depths of this well."
"What water? What well?"
"Who is it asking?"
Silence.
"What silence?"

ERNST KAISER & EITHNE WILKINS

From THE BOOK OF FORMATION:
10 COUNTINGS, WITH COMMENTARIES

יצירה

פרוש החץ

Call it a mist of light and sound a faint idea of interposition of being between dif-
down in it glowing round them joining them together as it holds them apart with
space between them packs in the bright steamy wool of white noise. The

יוצרות יוצריה

You must know that whatever was created in the universe was
which suggest the obscure root. Counting: that there may be
See: alef which is one begins, and bet which is two differs,
A space is cut free around the tongue
colors of the flame; not: the flame, the coal;

ספר יצירה

:A: With thirty-two wondrous ways of wisdom carved YH YHVH TSV'OT 'LHEY YSR'L 'LHIM HYIM 'L SHDAY and so created His Universe, with three sfr: with count and with recount and record.
:B: Ten countings of nothing in twenty-two marks on foundation....
:C: Ten countings of nothing. The number of ten fingers five and five, the covenant of the Only laid between like the tongue peeled out and like the penis peeled out.
:D: No more than ten...Set them then turn them back
:G: Ten countings of nothing. Their end inside their beginning, their beginning inside their end like the flame joined to the coal. That the Master is Only and has no Other, for before one how do you count?

ference which would otherwise not be. In the alef-bet of letters it sounds, Of sounds
weak energy swell of color where pulsing at the letter's edge the sound's shape
mists make the sounds and letters coherent; the beings, discrete.

created in man so that he might come to contemplate the secrets
differentiation. Recounting: marked by sounds and silences
gimel which is three makes endless; while one from gimel
language which divides the hands; a discretion
not the man then, but what the man is making.

the circle even inside the samekh immersed in it emergent from it sinking back
around empty ones emptiness of music whole words englobing words the
flame a man may follow to their source, or branches and leaves
is all the same though signs and sounds
ing nothing.
carving carves out man.   not: the many
nothing beneath. Nothing but   Only Making.

Nothing before, nothing after, nothing above
to divide the feet is the letter yod, ten, which man
leaves two and one for alef one count-
between. Recording; or by marks and spaces between the counting
of wisdom from what is apparent. And these ways are threads
forms darkness forms silence dams the ink rests the burden. Full letters
it is the image, Darkness of the light tone of silence. The letters arise within it cut

תולדות חיים

Schools of Sa'adia, the Rabad, the Ramban, fictions of Moshe Botarel; the Pride of Vilna. Ad loc.

(1) The *sefirot* (emanations) appear in the *Sefer Yetsira* in their earliest form, as numbers, quantities emerging from the void. This antedates the *sefirot* as descriptive qualities, etc. (see above, page 24) by many centuries. Thus the *Sefer Yetsira*, or *Book of Formation/Creation*, emphasizes number (*sfor*) as ground of the creative process, a kind of Jewish pythagoreanism that will not disappear but will later, in the mystical physics of the *Zohar*, be equated with light as energy, the universal constant of a possibly related physics in our own time. The book proceeds without explanations, goes from primal numbers in the opening section (printed here at center) to the 22 letters (numbers) of the Hebrew alphabet as constituents of the known world, & maintains sufficient condensation & tension to generate a whole literature derived from its images. But number & sound may also be read as the basis of any actual poetics. (For which, see below, page 228.)

The form of Lenowitz's assemblage "is modelled on the standard presentation of text and commentary in Hebrew religious books." (See also pages 78, 86.)

Albert Einstein (1879–1955)

E

---

mc^2

(Samaritan Hebrew)

THE TEN WORDS OF CREATION

In the beginning God created. And said
God, Let there be light. And God said,
Let there be a firmament. And God said, Let be collected
the waters. And God said, Bring forth grass
the earth. And God said, Let there be
lights. And God said, Let swarm
the water. And God said, Bring forth
the earth. And God said, Let us make
man. And God said, Behold I have given you.
And God saw all that
he had made, and behold it was very good. And he said, I
am the God of thy father, the God of Abraham
and the God of Isaac and the God of Jacob.
YHVH, YHVH, a God merciful and gracious, the Existent, YHVH.

JAMES A. MONTGOMERY

VARIATIONS ON GENESIS

(1) IN THE BEGINNING GOD CREATED THE HEAVEN
AND THE EARTH: you shouldn't read BERESHIT as *in the begin-
ning* but BERA SHIT, *He created six.* If the Writing says BERA SHIT,
that means he created six letters; and through them were the heavens and

the earth formed, as it is said: FOR THROUGH YH YHVH He formed the worlds. YH are two letters, YHVH are four, thus there are six. So you must understand that it is through six letters that God created the heavens and the earth. If you say, is it only the heavens and the earth that were created through these six letters, through the writing THROUGH YH YHVH HE FORMED THE WORLDS, understand as well that two worlds were created by these six letters: the world here and now, and the world that will be. (From *The Baraita of the Work of Creation.*)

(2) BY MEANS OF A BEGINNING IT CREATED GOD was zohar once again   because it sowed a seed would show its beauty like the silkworm self-enclosed in palace   made it for use & beauty   the Mysterious Unknown by means of this "beginning" made this palace   called it Elohim   (this god)   "by means of a beginning it created Elohim" (*Zohar:* Genesis 15a.)

(3) At the first of the gods' making skies and earth, the earth was a mixedup-darkness on top of deepness: so wind-of-the-gods swept down on the waters.
    The gods said LIGHT so there was light, and the gods liked the light so they made it different from the darkness:

> they called the light Day
> called the darkness Night:

> so that was Evening
> and that was Morning
> the first Day.

(Genesis 1.1 –.5.)

COMMENTARY

The "work of creation" appears here as continuous, a process uninterrupted by its codification in a literal text. Two points should be made: that the work of mything (& not simply as a fiction – "lie" – in Plato's sense) remains active to the present, & that the literal text itself, the act in this instance of biblical "genesis," is made to open again & again by re-reading, re-sounding, re-exegesis, in which the transmitted account is taken as an occasion for new departures, the mind & voice in constant motion. And this is the case exactly where we would have most expected stasis, frozen thought; or, as the *Zohar* tells it in the voice of Simeon bar Yoḥai: "The stories of the Torah are simply her outer garments, & woe to the man who looks on those garments as the Torah itself, for such a man will have no portion in the world to come. For David said: 'Open my eyes that I may behold wondrous things out of Thy law' [Psalm 119.18], i.e. the things beneath the garment."
    So also in the work of heretics & poets. A book of questions, changes.

(Hebrew, c. 8th century A.D.)

From THE PIRKE DE RABBI ELIEZER

. . . .

(1)

THE ORIGIN OF SKY

was from the light of his own robe
he took & stretched it
like a robe the skies
were rolling out from
he figured that should do it
in Shadai's words   "shall do"
– became his name then –
then firmed it up (they say)
"thy covering of thyself
"with light
"is like a robe
"the way thou stretchest the sky out
"'s like a curtain

(2)

THE ORIGIN OF EARTH

took snow or ice
– 'twas underneath his throne –
& dropped it on
the waters
then they became congealed
earth's crust was formed from it
(they say)
"he tells the snow
"be earth

J.R.

Said Rabbi Simeon: Mark this well! Fire, air, earth and water are the sources and roots of all things above and below, and all things above, below, are grounded in them. And in each of the four winds these elements are found – fire in the North, air in the East, water in the South, earth in the West; and the four elements are united with the four winds – and all are one. Fire, water, air and earth: gold, silver, copper and iron: north, south, east and west – altogether these make twelve; yet they are all one. (*Zohar: Exodus* 23b.)

Yannai (Hebrew, c. 6th century A.D.)

FIRE-POEM: "& THEN AN ANGEL OF THE LORD APPEARED TO HIM IN A TONGUE OF FIRE"

Fire eating
Fire carbonized in snow & smoke
Fire its look is like the face of
    mirrors
Fire flaring roaring

Fire flying in a storm wind
Fire every day renewal
Fire higher than its branches
Fire . . . .
Fire the iron bars of . . . .
Fire fevers in Sheol under
Fire black as raven

Fire burning dry & wet things
Fire of a crouching lion
Fire with assurance that it won't
    go out
Fire burns around turns back on
    self

Fire kindled without branches
Fire other fires don't swell out
Fire's sparks like lightning
Fire . . . .
Fire . . . .
Fire . . . .
Fire heaps of color like the rainbow

*

. . . & changes image crowds on image
on the Burning Bush in flames
Sinai with torches
overhead were kindling sparks
below it licking light rays
inside it the domain of seraphim
who aren't burnt thereby
& from the sweat they sweat

a fire river conduit of light
whose sinews are nodules   snow
the fire doesn't boil off snow
is itself not doused by snow
for fire's maker snow's creator
ordered peace between the fire & snow
o judgment by fire o judgment by snow

J.R. / H.L.

COMMENTARY

"It is a well-known fact that the Master of the Book Yetsira described the right-hand side, Our Lady of Mercy & Compassion, as water, since everything needs water; & as the Master of the Book Yetsira described the right-hand side as water, so he described the left-hand side as fire." (Moses of Burgos, *Sefer Amud ha-Smoli*, or the Book of the Left Pillar.)

Eleazar ha-Kallir (Hebrew, 7th century A.D.)

WATER-POEM: A PRAYER & INVOCATION TO THE PRINCE OF RAIN

Af-Bri
      sign
            name of
                      rain's angel
clouding
        vaporing
                emptying
                        raining
sprouts
        of water
                crown
                      this valley
won't stop
        compact
                goes on
                      unyielding

shielding them
                    faithful
                                beggars for
                                            rain

& you my hero forever Yahveh my god you wake the dead many times you
save us

be watchful
                    send down
                                    rain from
                                                    rain rivers
melt
        the face of
                            earth
                                    with clear opals
water
        your power
                        your mark
                                        written down
like drops
                reviving
                            those who blow
                                                breath
you restore
                who invoke
                                powers of
                                                rain

.   .   .   .

(invocation thru the fathers priests & tribes)

: our Elohim & Elohim of our fathers
remember the father
                            you drew behind you
                                                        like water
you blessed like a tree
                                planted by streams
                                                    of water
you shielded
                    saved him from fire
                                        & water

you would guard
                    when he seeded beside
                                        every water
because of him don't stop your water

remember words of his birth
                    let him drink
                                        the small water
you told his father to kill him
                                        his blood spilt
                                                            like water
as he was ready to spill
                                        his heart
                                                            like water
to dig & to find
                    wells
                                        of water
because of him pour down your water

remember
                    who carried his stick across
                                        Jordan's water
one-hearted
                    rolled stones from the mouth of the well
                                                            of water
when he wrestled the prince
                                        mixed from fire
                                                            & water
till you promised
                    you would stay with him
                                        in fire & in water
because of him don't stop your water

remember the one they drew out
                                        from a reed boat
                                                            in the water
they commanded
                    & didn't he water his flock
                                                            with water
the people you chose
                    when they thirsted
                                        for water

he beat on the rock
                    it opened & gave out
                                        water
because of him pour down your water

remember the temple priest
                    who bathed 5 times
                                        in water
who walked
            who washed his hands in holiness
                                        of water
reading
        sprinkling purifying
                    water
kept distant
            from a people violent
                            as water
because of him don't stop your water

remember the 12 tribes
                    you made to cross
                                the water
for whom you sweetened
                    bitterness
                            of water
whose generations
                spilt their blood for you
                                like water
o turn our minds
            encircled by
                    that water
because of them pour down your water

for you are Yahveh are our elohim you make the wind blow & the rain fall
down

                                                    J.R. / H.L.

COMMENTARY

"Water is the original glyph of the universe, and what occurs in the hoary bosom of
the sea will divulge far more to man than the knowledge of the ground and its veg-
etation." (Edward Dahlberg, *Reasons of the Heart,* 1965.)

(Hebrew, 4th / 5th centuries A.D.)

From THE BOOK OF MYSTERIES   "Rites for the Sun"

FOURTH HEAVEN heaven of the angels of the sun lies stretched out
in a storm wind stands on fire pillars wearing crowns of flame is filled with
storage chambers of the powers treasuries of dew & angels in the corners
lightly gallop gallop & in it there are seven rivers fire water & beside them
angels standing on both sides are numberless

from this side fire angels burning flames & on the other water angels frozen
into hail they do not put each other out do not ignite each other but these
dip in the fire rivers those dip in the water rivers calling making songs &
praises to the one who lives forever made them to express his strength

& this heaven houses the sun's canopy is full of light & fires come together
fire angels ringed with power who surround him drive him through the day
& water angels bodies like the sea their voice is like the voice of water fierce
with beauty drive him through the night

                    .   .   .   .

if you long to see the sun by day easy in his chariot & rising watch & guard
yourself & purify yourself for 7 days avoid all victuals & all drink & every-
thing unclean

& on the 7th day stand before him in the hour that he rises make a smoke
before him an incense of spices 3 shekels in weight & call on the names of
angels 7 times who drive him through the day & if these don't answer 7
times go back & call them backwards 7 times & say

I CALL ON YOU ANGELS WHO DRIVE THE SUN YOUR
ENERGY YOUR POWERS DRIVING THE SKY ROAD
THAT ILLUMINATES THE WORLD BY HIM WHOSE
VOICE SHAKES THE EARTH WHO SHIFTS MOUN-
TAINS IN HIS ANGER HAS STRENGTH TO CALM THE
SEA HIS GLANCE WOBBLES THE PILLARS OF THE
WORLD WHO CARRIES UNIVERSES ON HIS ARM IN-
VISIBLE TO EYE OR ANY LIVING THING WHO SITS

UPON THE THRONE OF GREATNESS OF THE KING-
DOM OF THE KABOD OF HIS HOLY HOLY ROAMING
OF THE WHOLE WORLD BY HIS NAME O GREAT O
TERRIBLE O BRAVE O HUGE O FIERCE O POWERFUL
O HOLY O STRONG O WONDERFUL O HIDDEN O
RAISED UP O LUMINOUS I CALL YOU BACK & CALL
ON YOU TO DO MY WILL MY LONGING AT THIS
TIME & SEASON TO REMOVE THE CENTER OF THE
SUN ITS CORE THAT I MAY SEE HIM FACE TO FACE
THE WAY HE IS BENEATH HIS CANOPY & LET ME
NOT CATCH FIRE FROM YOUR FIRE BUT GIVE HIM
LEAVE TO DO MY WILL

& when you finish calling you will see the sun under the canop will ask if life
or death will follow or if good or evil when you seek to send the sun back
then remember your first oath & say

I CALL ON YOU RETURN THE SUN'S CORE TO ITS
PLACE THE WAY IT WAS & MAY THE SUN GO ON ITS
WAY

. . . .

if you long to see the sun at night & going on a northern path purify yourself
3 weeks of 7 days avoid all victuals & all drink & everything unclean stand at
the night watch the third hour & wrapped in white cloth speak the sun's
name & the names of angels 21 times those who drive him through the
night & say

I CALL ON YOU ANGELS FLYING IN THE AIR ALONG
THE FIRMAMENT BY HIM WHO SEES UNSEEN HIM-
SELF THE KING REVEALING EVERYTHING UNSEEN
WHO SEES ALL HIDDEN THINGS THE CHIEF WHO
KNOWS THE SECRETS OF THE DARKNESSES WHO
TURNS DEEP DARKNESS INTO MORNING MAKES
NIGHT AS LIGHT AS DAY ALL HIDDEN THINGS
MADE KNOWN BEFORE HIM LIKE THE SUN & NOTH-
ING IS TOO WONDERFUL FOR HIM & BY HIS NAME
THE HOLY KING WHO GLIDES ON WINGS OF WIND &
BY THE LETTERS OF HIS SECRET NAME REVEALED
TO ADAM IN THE GARDEN RULES CONSTELLA-
TIONS & THE SUN & MOON BOW DOWN LIKE SER-
VANTS TO THEIR MASTER BY THE NAME OF HIM

THE GOD OF WONDERS NOW I CALL ON YOU TO
MAKE KNOWN THIS GREATER MIRACLE & LET ME
SEE THE SUN IN POWER IN THE COMPLEX WORK-
INGS OF HIS WHEELS NO PORTION OF THESE UN-
SEEN THINGS TOO WONDROUS FOR MY EYES A
WHOLE DAY LET ME SEE IT ASK HIM WHAT I LONG
FOR LET HIM SPEAK WITH ME THE WAY A MAN
SPEAKS WITH HIS FRIEND TO TELL ME SECRETS OF
THE DEPTHS MAKE KNOWN THE HIDDEN THINGS
TO ME BUT NOTHING BAD TO HAPPEN NOTHING
BAD

& as you finish speaking you will hear a voice the thunder from the north &
something will appear like lightning worlds will shine before you you will
see it & bow down & falling earthwards on your face will pray this prayer

(a Greek hymn for Helios the sun god)

I ADORE YOU HELIOS
        CLIMBING THE EAST
GOOD SAILOR
KEEPING THE FAITH
HIGH DRIVER
LONG AGES YOU PRIMED YOUR GREAT GLOBE
O HOLY ASSEMBLER
YOU GOVERN THE MESSENGERS
LORD
SHINING DRIVER
KING WHO SETS OUT THE STARS

& I PLONY BEN PLONY HURL MY PLEAS AT YOU MAY
YOU BE SEEN BY ME REVEALED TO ME UNFRIGHT-
ENED NOTHING EVER BE CONCEALED FROM ME
BUT EVERYTHING I ASK YOU SPEAK

then stand on your feet you will see him up north moving east & turning
your hands back behind you & bending your head will ask him everything
then raise your eyes up to the sky & say

URPALI'EL I CALL ON YOU BY HIM WHO MADE YOU
FOR HIS GLORY & HIS MAJESTY MADE YOU TO
LIGHT HIS WORLD TO RULE HIS WORLD THAT YOU

NOT DAMAGE ME NOT FRIGHTEN ME THAT I NOT
BE AFRAID OR TREMBLE & YOU TURN BACK ALONG
YOUR ROAD IN PEACE REVOLVING THAT YOU NOT
BE KEPT FROM MOTION NOW & FOR ALL TIME
AMEN SELAH

J.R. / H.L.

COMMENTARY

The worship of the sun – & other powers of earth & sky – persists in spite of efforts to desacralize the image in favor of the one god. The Hebrew word for sun is *shemesh,* sun-god of the Babylonians, whose cult Ezekiel spies out in the Temple, still vivid as a memory of same in later ritual; thus, after Patai, *Man & Temple:* "at the Eastern Gate / they looked back / said / 'our fathers stood here / backs turned to the temple / faces east / & bowed before the Sun.'" But the text adds later: "As for us, our eyes are turned to the Lord."

Yet the issue, in popular, magical & meditative Judaism, is (like much other nature-related mythopoeia) far less resolved than that. The Greek prayer to Helios, above, is transcribed in Hebrew letters & is part of a widespread Jewish & Hellenistic convergence. Of a roughly contemporary manifestation, E. R. Goodenough writes: "We have all along known that the Essenes addressed prayers to the sun." And in the fragment from the Dead Sea scrolls that follows, two other astrological beings appear among the constellations – to remind us of the abundance of such in the ongoing Jewish *poesis.*

(Hebrew, c. 1st century A.D.)

THE CODE OF DAY & NIGHT   "A Fragment"

---

(1)

* * . . .

h . . .

. . . .
& a man who would become. . . . .
broad & rounded . . .
mixed & not the flesh of . . .

(2)

. . . . unclean
. . . . hard stone
. . . . a man of . . .
. . . . . clean
& thighs are long & thin & toes
are thin & long was from the second vault
spends 6 parts in the house of light 3 in the pit
of darkness is his time of birth the festival
of taurus will grow poor his beast is taurus

(3)

wa * h . . . .
& the head . . . .
of terror . . . wingy teeth & fingers of
his hands are thick thighs thick & hairy
toes are thick & short spends 8 parts in the house
of darkness 1 part in the house of light a man . . .

J.R.

COMMENTARY

Here the original message was written down in code: "a cipher [that used] the comparatively simple expedient of reversing the order of the letters of the words & employing a combination of alphabets." (J. M. Allegro, "An Astrological Cryptic Document from Qumran.") The resort to cryptography was symptomatic: a move from an open relationship with sky & stars to a hidden one, in which the old images had become not only awesome but demonic: the natural world a presence man must defeat & master, or with which he must traffic outside the law, in secret. Writes Robert Kelly of "that wisdom outlawed & made criminal by the city of Rome," etc., a condition of separation suffered by the Jews as well: "The traditional sciences became 'occult' when the city took on its modern sense. . . . Just as the sky over a modern city is occulted by smoke & industrial throwaway, its proper atmosphere, so that antique science based on the inspection of the sky becomes mythologized, & hence a fossilized, hence a despised, science, rather than an open possibility. . . . There are no ready pragmatic ways of inferring the Pleiades. They go unseen, their dance ignored. And we are cut off."

This is the condition of the lost garden, as also of the city deprived of its cosmic model, etc., still to be sighted in the coded poem; for which, in the variety of their Jewish manifestations, see page 232, below.

MENORAH

1   she lights the lights

2   the bridegroom moves to her

3   the tree of life
     is upside down

4   the sun

5   illumination of the bride

6   whose light is sarah

7   lighting fires

     making love

COMMENTARY

(1) The tree of life, which represents the mystery of consciousness & link, or ladder, between earth & sky, appears here as the menorah or great seven-branched candelabrum of the Jewish temple. Thus the earthly tree is also sky tree, whose seven lamps were long ago read as the seven planets: "the eyes of Yahveh looking on the earth," the book says (Zechariah 4.10). Yet the latent imagery is also strongly sexual, for the tree's sap, which fed the lamps of the menorah, is elsewhere seen as semen, blood, or milk, the true *elixir vitae*. And this is acknowledged in the accompanying rituals, from the strenuous, near acrobatic movements of the temple priests who climbed ladders to fill & light the bowls with wicks made from the High Priest's underwear, to the domestic candle-lighting of each sabbath, which Safed kabbalists & others celebrated as a marriage between God & his bride: "an almost complete identification of the *Shekhinah*, not only with the Queen of the Sabbath, but also with every Jewish housewife who celebrates the Sabbath" (G. Scholem). *She who lights the lights.*

(2) Elsewhere the tree of life – in vision of the Samaritan messiah & "first gnostic," Simon Magus – contains the child of light & heat (= messiah = the anointed one with oil of olives). And it is imaged also in the Garden mysteries, the burning bush as seen by Moses, the menorah of the Jewish temple, the cross that passes into Christian cult, the sefirotic "tree" of the kabbala. In *poesis*, which is itself the *ma'ase*

bereshit ("work of creation" as renewed beginning), the tree is consciousness, the brain & spinal tree inside us, at whose base the serpent (= yoga "kundalini") waits. Writes Gaston Bachelard: "The imagination is a tree. It has the integrative virtues of a tree. It is root and boughs. It lives between earth and sky. It lives in the earth and in the wind. The imagined tree imperceptibly becomes the cosmological tree, the tree which epitomizes a universe, which makes a universe." This is the tree of the first garden: two trees united (in another telling) that the fall of man, our entry into (or away from) consciousness divides, creates a schism between mind & knowledge, as burden of the severed intellect, beginnings of abstraction.

Nathan of Gaza (Hebrew, c. 1643–80)

SERPENT

Messiah.

(by *gematria*)

COMMENTARY

(1) Like the cosmologies of Naasene & Sethian gnostics (circa third century A.D.), the works of heterodox mystics like Nathan of Gaza (see below, page 138) give contrastive views of the serpent as destroyer/preserver. In its positive sense the event in the garden is the bringing of knowledge (gnosis); thus the related Ophites: "We venerate the Serpent ... cause of Gnosis for mankind." Suppressed in Judaism—as by other prevailing orthodoxies—the idea never wholly disappears.

(2) "Know & believe that the Serpent, at the beginning of creation, was indispensable to the order of the world. . . . It is he who moves the spheres & turns them from East to the West & from the North to the South. Without him there would have been neither seed nor germination, nor will to produce any created thing." (Joseph Gikatilla, *Mystery of the Serpent*, c. 1300.)

Harris Lenowitz (b. 1945)

THE WIND   TWO TREES   MEN AND WOMEN

Shabbes Bereshis: for Tamar

Ruah elohim *wind of god* / *nefesh haya living* / *breath living creature* / neshama *the wind soft-* / *blowing huffed into the* / *Adam* Yahweh *the* / *puffer comes to visit the* / *Adam   a friendly call* le- / ruah ha-yom *at the* / *breezy part of the day just* / *towards evening* ruah / elohim   nefesh ne- / shama   Yahweh leruah / ha-yom *a warm breath* / *bound on hare hare's* / *breath in wind   the wind* / *carries spoor* Va-yikra / yahweh elohim el ha- / adam *Yahweh of the gods* / *calls the Adam   to serve* / *Yahweh knows where the* / *Adam   is   to   service* / *passing for fate   to*

The woman sees that the tree provides good food, is easy on the eyes and charms toward wisdom, takes of its fruit and eats, also giving some to her man with her and he eats   The eyes of both of them open and they know they are naked (eyrumim) They sew fig-leaf into belts for themselves They hear the voice of Yahweh going about in the garden at the breezy time of the day (le-ruah ha-yom) and the Adam and his woman hide from the face of Yahweh of the gods among the trees of the garden   Yahweh of the gods calls to the Adam "Where are you?" And he answers, "I heard your voice in the garden, was afraid because I was naked (eyrom) and hid" So He said, "Who told you you were naked? Have you eaten from the I-commanded-you-not-to-eat-from-it tree?" The Adam said, "The woman you presented to be with me   she presented me from the tree and I ate"

memory zikharon *of ruin-will-be*   zakhar *is* zikharon *man is memory Now naked*   eyrom   the Adam *sees his prick*   zakhar   *and the woman's hole* (isha *woman   one breath longer than   man* ish) (*her man* ishah)   they are naked   now know they are naked   their knowledge is arum *subtile   they are* eyrum *naked Yahweh pants after them pants after him   the Adam   the knows remembering*   zakhar   arom eyrum   va-yipah be-apav nish-mat hayim   va-yehi ha-adam le-nefesh haya   *when Yahweh of the gods huffed breath to life* zakhar u-nekeva *prickandhole he made them   but before* naase adam be-tsalmeynu ki-dmuteynu . . . va-yivra elohim et ha-adam be-tsalmo be-tselem elohim bara oto *in his image he made him/it The god is woman/man the Adam was lonely couldn't find a completion a perfection an incompletion sleight of hand makes two halves more than one whole forget go to deepsleep* va-yapeyl Yahweh elohim tardema al ha-adam *forget Creation imperfect by design! Correct it the very try is evil is good From* basar ehad *one flesh two flesh two bone the Adam CHOOSES* ve-davak be-ishto *to stick by his own bone gives up*

But recalls in the breezy evening to Thou a fix plan says ha-isha asher natata imadi hi natna li min ha-eyts va-okheyl *she gave me it the one you gave to be with me Rabbit flashing teeth no alibi no excuses no forgiveness challenge We are man we remember we are one for all your test It will do me in But I remember why You failed feared tricked And Yahweh of the gods cannot still the voice or the wind fears his image the power of himself knowing himself like the man knows the woman remembering other battles other gods:* va-y omer Yahweh elohim heyn ha-adam haya ke-ahad mi-menu la-daat tov va-ra ve-ata pen yishlah yado ve-lakah gam me-eyts ha-hayim ve-akhal va-hay le-olam va-yeshalheyhu Yahweh elohim mi-gran eyden *Keep him now he knows from being one of us living forever*

The Evil sits still with the Good Yahweh elohim is one Even with the help of man granting logos shekhina can never be two trying to be one The man and the woman have their halfdom knitting together melting making the old One bringing more to make Onetry knowing remembering when making game of harehound

COMMENTARY

from "the notebooks" 12/75 for Harris Lenowitz & as a prologue to the Book of Job

o has the work of creation ended?
ended & plunged us into terror
eye of your god still lurking there
like snake in its hole
mad snake
when will you strike again & be beautiful
& shining like the rainbow

sign of god & peace   you who were meant to be man's lover   (the old texts
say)   *our houses full of cherished snakes   high beings   angels with cocks &
eyes*   o the dream of the voluptuary is still   still true   the snake still
splendid in   world of his emanations   your mysteries no less than ours
you prince of coils   of circles   urge to make life that drives you snake as well
      o impulse to create   to be prolific   & the good (they said) rests on this
evil too   what's at the center then?   the face of the devourer   blood-
smeared face stares back at us across our terror   auschwitz   hiroshima
& we ask   who are the panthers in the temple?   what is the pain Job feels
      & why?   the answer   S I L E N C E   until the mute man cries   in self-
denial   makes his god speak through madness   as the wind of Yahveh

yammered
called to Job
o has the work of creation ended?
in clash of contraries
it starts again
the words of Yahveh raised against us
for you have not spoken of me
the thing that is true
as my servant Job hath
in which the work resumes

(j.r.)

Louis Zukofsky (1904–1978)

THE IYYOB TRANSLATION FROM "A-15"

An
   hinny
by
   stallion
out of
   she-ass

He neigh ha lie low h'who y'he gall mood
So roar cruel hire
Lo to achieve an eye leer rot off
Mass th'lo low o loam echo
How deal me many coeval yammer
Naked on face of white rock — sea.
Then I said: Liveforever my nest
Is arable hymn
Shore she root to water
Dew anew to branch.

Wind: Yahweh at Iyyob
Mien His roar 'Why yammer
Measly make short hates oh
By milling bleat doubt?
Eye sore gnaw key heaver haul its core
Weigh as I lug where hide any?
If you — had you towed beside the roots?
How goad Him — you'd do it by now —
My sum My made day a key to daw?
O Me not there allheal — a cave.

All mouth deny hot bough?
O me you're raw — Heaven pinned Dawn stars
Brine I heard choir and weigh by care —
Why your ear would call by now Elohim:
Where was soak — bid lot tie in hum —
How would you have known to hum
How would you all oats rose snow lay
Assay how'd a rock light rollick ore
Had the rush in you curb, ah bay,
But the shophar yammer *heigh horse'*

Wind: Yahweh at Iyyob 'Why yammer,'
Wind: Iyyob at Yahweh 'Why yammer
How cold the mouth achieved echo.'
Wind: Yahweh at Iyyob 'Why yammer

Ha neigh now behēmoth and share I see see your make
Giddy pair – stones – whose rages go
Weigh raw all gay where how spill lay who'
Wind: Iyyob
'Rain without sun hated? *hurt no one*
In two we shadow, how hide any.'

THE END OF "A BOOK OF WORLDS"

ב

THE VISIONS

Nothing, only an image, nothing else, utter oblivion.
Slanting through the words come vestiges of light.
— FRANZ KAFKA

If you are "my witnesses," I am the Lord
& if you are not my witnesses
I am not, as it were, the Lord
— SIMEON BAR YOḤAI

A Book of Beards

Gertrude Stein (1874–1946)

From PATRIARCHAL POETRY

Their origin and their history patriarchal poetry their origin and their history patriarchal poetry their origin and their history.

Patriarchal Poetry.

Their origin and their history.

Patriarchal Poetry their origin and their history their history patriarchal poetry their origin patriarchal poetry their history their origin patriarchal poetry their history patriarchal poetry their origin patriarchal poetry their history their origin.

That is one case.

Able sweet and in a seat.

Patriarchal poetry their origin their history their origin. Patriarchal poetry their history their origin.

(Hebrew, Bible, c. 10th century B.C.)

From THE BOOK OF GENESIS "Akeda"

with commentaries by H.L., et al.

ספר האגדה **בראשית כב וירא**

"he took his two servants/boys with him (G. 22.4)" – That is, Ishmael and Eliezer. He said: 'While I'm sacrificing him they can watch the equipment.' A contention arose between them, and Ishmael said: 'Now Father's sacrificing Isaac his son for an 'ola, I being his first-born son, I will be his inheritor.' Eliezer said to him, 'He's already driven you off to the desert; but I am his servant, having served his house day and night – I am the heir' And the Holy Spirit answered: 'This one will not inherit and neither will the other. Don't be ridiculous.' "He saw the place/ Place from a distance (G.22.4)" How did it look from a distance? What was seen from a distance? This phrase teaches us that in the beginning it was a deep place, but when the Holy-One-Blessed-Is-He commanded that his Presence should be settled there and the place made a Holy Place, he thought: 'It is not the fashion for a king to dwell in a valley but on a high place, raised up and beautified, visible to all. Immediately thereafter the Holy-One-

After these things Elohim tested Avraham. He called, 'Avraham,' who answered, 'I am here.' He said, 'Take now your son, your only, the one you've loved. Yitshak. Go over to the Moria land and offer him up as a burnt offering on the hill I show you.' So Avraham got up early in the morning, saddled his donkey and got his two servants and his son Yitshak together. He broke up some wood for the offering and left quickly for the place the Elohim had told him of. Three days later, Avraham caught sight of the place from a distance. Avraham took the firewood and put it on his son Yitshak; he himself carried the fire and cleaver. The two of them went on together.

Yitshak asked his father, 'My father?,' and he said, 'I am here, my son.' Then Yitshak said, 'The fire and wood for the burnt offering are here, but where is the sheep?' Avraham answered, 'Elohim will see to the sheep for the offering, my son.' The two of them continued on together.

They came to the place Elohim had mentioned, and Avraham built the altar and laid out the wood. He bound his son Yitshak, and laid him on the altar on top of the wood. Avraham put out his hand and picked up the cleaver, ready to slaughter his son. Then a messenger from Y H V H /Elohim/ called to him from the sky, 'Avraham, Avraham.' Avraham said, 'I am here,' and the messenger went on. 'Do not put your hand on the boy. Do nothing to him. I know well now that you respect Elohim, for you have not hidden even your son, your only one, from me.' Avraham caught sight of a /different/ ram caught in the hedge by his horns. He took it up and offered it as a burnt offering instead of his son. Avraham named that place 'Y H V H sees to it'; the mountain is today called 'Y H V H may be seen.'

Blessed-Is-He gestured to the surroundings of the valley that they should gather together into one place in order to provide a setting for his Presence. Abraham said to Isaac: – 'Do you see what I see?' He answered him: 'I see a pleasant hill, glorious with a cloud clinging around it.' He asked his servants/boys: 'Do you see anything?' They answered him: 'We only see wastelands.' He said to them: 'Asininities! You are just like the ass which sees something but doesn't know what he sees. "stay here with the ass (G. 22.5)"'

"An angel of God called to him from the skies, 'Abraham, Abraham'" (G. 22.1) like someone calling in trouble. Abraham turned towards him. The angel said to him: 'What are you doing? "Don't lay a hand on the boy! (G.22.12)"' Abraham asked him: 'Who are You?' He answered: 'I'm an angel' Abraham said to him: 'When the Holy-One-Blessed-Is-He ordered me to sacrifice my son he himself told me, so now if he wants something else He will order it. Thereupon the Holy-One-Blessed-Is-He opened the

Then the messenger of Y H V H called Avraham again from the sky. He said, 'I am sworn – it is a speech of Y H V H – that since you have done this thing – not even holding back your son, your only one – that I will bless you in every smallest thing, and make your seed so many as the stars of the skies and the grains of sand on the edge of the sea. Your seed will take the gate of their enemies. All the nations of the earth will be blessed through your seed because you have listened to me.'

Avraham returned to his servants, and they all left together for Seven Wells. Avraham settled down at Seven Wells.

firmament and the cloud and said to him: "I swear it on myself (G.22.17)"' Abraham said to him: 'You have sworn and I too swear that I will not go down from this altar until I've said all I must say.' He said to him: 'Speak,' Abraham said to him: 'Didn't you say to me, "Your seed will be like the number of the stars (G.15.5)"?' The Holy-One-Blessed-Is-He answered: 'Yes.' He (A.) asked him: 'Through whom?' He answered: 'Through Isaac.' He (A.) said to him: 'When you said to me "Offer him for an 'ola" I could have recalled your promise to you but I overcame my inclination to do so; in order that Isaac's sons, when they enter into trouble or sin might be redeemed on behalf of the binding of Isaac and that it might be remembered by you just as if his dust lay heaped on the altar; and that you might be merciful and forgive them and redeem them from their trouble.' The Holy-One-Blessed-Is-He said to him: 'You have said your piece, now I will say mine: Isaac's sons will sin against me and I will judge them at the New Year, but if they entreat that I might seek credit for them I will remember in their behalf the binding of Isaac – if they sound the shofar from this one.' He asked him: 'What shofar?' He answered him: 'Turn around ... ' Thereupon "He raised his eyes and looked and there was a ram ... (G.22.13)" R. Eliezer says: 'He came from the mountains; was grazing there.' R. Yehoshua says: 'An angel brought him from The Garden of Eden where he was grazing beneath the tree of life and drinking from the waters that run beneath it, and his fragrance diffused throughout the world. When was he set in the Garden? Between the suns of the six days of creation.'

פרוש החץ

The words tell the story by seven of seeing   to look six times and once respect   in the root that means 'see-and-respect' resh-'alef-yod = yod-resh-'alef   Once is the Land of Seeing   moria' once Avraham sees the Place   va-yar' 'et ha-makom   once is Elohim will see to the sheep himself'   elohim yire'lo   once Avraham sees Elohim and has respect forever yare' 'elohim 'ata   immediately va-yar' ve-hine 'ayil Avraham sees the ram at the place Avraham calls 'Y H V H sees to it'   Y H V H yire'   and we call 'Y H V H can be seen to'   Y H V H yera'e   that is the Hill of Seeing Moriah

And here there is more: 'al tikra' 'Read not' yahdav three times 'together' twice 'the two of them went on together' once and 'and they all left together' but rather yahzu 'the two of them went on they were seeing' twice and 'and they all left seeing'   Read not 'for you have not withheld your son' ela' 'but rather' 'for you have not darkened your son from the seeing' ki lo' hashakhta'   And what is it the story tells? Only how Avraham and Elohim saved Yitshak arranged for mercy and taught how to see   to those who do see   only by keeping their eyes on one another   and by looking out each for the other

Akeda = (Hebrew) "binding" – "referring to Abraham's binding of his son Isaac on an altar on Mt. Moriah as an intended sacrifice in obedience to God's command" (*The New Jewish Encyclopedia*). (Thus: the putative beginnings of normative patriarchal Judaism.) Lenowitz's treatment of text & commentary (inherited & personal) is traditional in both its form & content.

(Hebrew, 2nd century B.C.)

From THE TESTAMENTS OF THE 12 PATRIARCHS
"Joseph & the Bull"

> *& Joseph dreamed & told it to his brothers (said) see I have dreamed*
> *a dream: & see the sun & moon & the 11 stars bow down to me: &*
> *told it to his father & his brothers: & his father turned on him & said:*
> *what is this dream you dreamed? shall I & shall your mother & your*
> *brothers come to you & bow down to the earth?*
> (Genesis 37.9 – .10.)

words of our father Jacob (said)
    my sons   run everywhere
    grab what your hands can hold
    thrust in my sight
we thought   said
    what can we make our own?
    we only see
        the sun
            the moon
                the stars
he said
    whatever your hands can hold
Levi first grabbed a stick
he raised it up
jumped on the sun

& rode it
which Judah saw
he saw him
raised a stick himself
then rode the moon
the nine tribes followed each one
rode his star his planet
in the sky
   left only Joseph
on the earth
our father Jacob said
  my son why did you not do
  what your brothers did
he thought said
  I am a man
    born to a woman not
      sky's child
  my end will be
    returning standing
      back on earth
& speaking looked he saw
a great bull near him
wings were like a stork's
his horns the reem's horns
Jacob said
  you mount him Joseph son
  you ride upon his back
which Joseph did
he mounted on the bull
when Jacob left him
Joseph then rode four hours gloried
in the bull the bull
flew up with him his hand
reached for a stick
started to strike his brothers

              J.R.

As elsewhere the "sons of Israel" are both individuals & tribes. The dream of Joseph takes us backward to a world of gods & titans: the elders towering in childhood visions. Within his dream-time world, the man as hero moves among the stars, plays out a ritual in which the possible is real, the wish fulfilled. The brothers are the founders, sons-of-origin, & one of them (the chief) recalls still how the human line goes back to earth. And hidden in that line the secret of the totem shows the tribes related to the other children of the earth. These are the animal-powers, summoned elsewhere in the praises of the fathers, as when Jacob names his sons in blessing them (Genesis 49, J Document); thus Judah as a lion's whelp, Issachar as a rawboned ass, Dan as a roadside serpent, Naphtali as a hind, and Joseph as a "wild colt by a spring."

A PROLOGUE TO THE WORKS OF MOSES

. . . .

Moses said: "I am only flesh & blood & cannot look upon the angels." But the angel Metatron changed Moses' tongue into a tongue of fire, & his eyes he made like the wheels of the heavenly chariot, & his power like that of the angels, & his tongue like a flame, & brought him up to heaven. 15,000 angels were on the right hand & 15,000 on the left, Metatron & Moses in the middle.

Eleazar ben Judah of Worms (Hebrew, c. 1176–1238)
THE IMAGE OF SPEECH AT SINAI

the Creator lowered fire on the mountain   great glorious magnificent
they say   *Mount Sinai was completely smoke for YaHVeH dropped on it in fire*
surrounded it with cloud & mist & darkness   a black cloud   they say
made darkness his hiding place   the voice mixed with fire & the voice came
out in fire   image of the voice seen in a cloud   a word emerging chiseled
in its bounds a letter wavered in the air   the people saw the speech the im-
age of the letters   then they knew that he was carving light from darkness
    because the fire blazed   it flamed like light that breaks out of the sur-
rounding dark   they say   *YaHVeH speaking to you from middle of the fire*
thus   as if a man was speaking to you on a cold day letters coming from his
mouth & cutting up the air to leave their image   when he spoke at Sinai *you
could hear his voice then in middle of the fire*   thus   an inner fire that burned
beside his speech   *the flowering of your word illumines* wrapped in darkness
so they could not see the voice the speech would enter in the hearer's heart
    & then he thought he heard the voice speak mouth to mouth   thus:

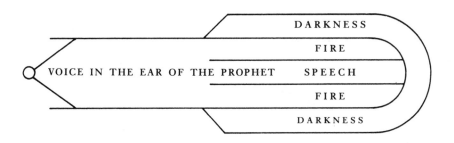

DARKNESS
FIRE
VOICE IN THE EAR OF THE PROPHET   SPEECH
FIRE
DARKNESS

J.R. / H.L.

(1) "Now Moses would stand and the word would come into his ear as through some sort of pipe, so that none other of the Children of Israel could hear it. When Moses' face flushed, however, they knew that the word had come to him." (*Pesikta Rabati*, 5.11.)

(2) "The Patriarchs, and especially Moses, are [according to Philo] the great revelation of the higher Way. . . . Each reveals a different aspect of the struggle to rise, or of mystic achievement. But each Patriarch is really one who has achieved the end of the Mystery. . . . The Mystery of Moses abandoned the material world and led the worshiper above all material association; he died to the flesh, and in becoming reclothed in a spiritual body moved progressively upward through the *kosmos noetos*, the Powers, and at last ideally to God himself, being at each stage identified with the spiritual existence at that stage. . . . Moses, who put off his physical nature, went into the darkness naked, and so had communion in a constant way with the Monad, as a result of which he became the true initiate, hierophant of the rites, and teacher of divine things." (E. R. Goodenough, *By Light, Light*, pages 96, 238, describing Philo's view of Judaism as a mystery religion, centered in "initiation.")

(Hebrew, Bible, c. 12th century B.C.)

From THE BOOK OF EXODUS   "Song of the Sea"

---

now Moses & now Israel's children sing this song
to Yahveh   saying
I would sing this song to YAHVEH
                    glorious in glory
   horse & rider hurled into the sea
my strength my song are YAHVEH
victory is YAHVEH
      THIS ONE is my god
            I give my field to
         is my father's gods
            I raise him up
YAHVEH is a man of war
YAHVEH's name is YAHVEH
      pharaoh's chariots
                  his army

                    hurled into the sea
          his master drivers
                    sinking   in   the   reed   sea
                                        red sea
's deeps have covered them
they drop into its shadows like a stone
          your right hand
                    YAHVEH
          beautiful with power
          your right hand
                    YAHVEH
          shatters your enemies
& by your endlessness of glories
those who stand against you
                    you put down
your anger issues
               you eat them up
                    like straw
& by the winds your nostrils blow
the waters gathered
          stood
               became a flowing hill
depths clotting in the heart of sea
the enemy had said
          I will pursue them
               I will catch them
                    I will divide the spoils
          my life will be fulfilled in them
               my sword be bare
                    my hand be their inheritor
you blew them with your wind
          the sea has covered them
               they sink like lead in mighty waters
who is like you
          YAHVEH
          among the gods
who is like you
               strong   withdrawn
                    feared in our praises
                         doing wonders
you bent down your right hand
          earth ate them up

                    A BOOK OF BEARDS / 93

became our lead in kindness
            took this people to you
you our guide in power
                to your holy field
the people heard
            would tremble
writhing of the people of Philistia
the chiefs of Edom shaken up
the gods of Moab chattering
men of Canaan melted
fear & terror on their heads
the power of your arm has made them
            still as any stone
until your people has passed over
            YAHVEH
when this people has passed over
                whom you bought
            you bring
            you plant them
on the mountain
            your inheritance
a place set up
        for you to sit in
a place you worked
        a holy place of ADONAI our masters
            your hands set up
                o YAHVEH
YAHVEH will be king
o world o time

                    (coda)

& Miriam the seer Aaron's sister
took drum in hand
the other women moved behind her
beating drums & dancing
Miriam responded
"sing to YAHVEH
            "glorious in glory
        "horse & rider hurled into the sea
"my strength my song are YAHVEH

                                    J.R. / H.L.

"We have been taught that every one who sings this hymn daily with true devotion will be worthy to sing it at the Redemption that is to be, for it refers both to the past world & to the future world. . . . The Shekinah will sing this song to the Lord, because the King will receive Her with a radiant countenance." (*Zohar: Exodus* 54b.)

(Hebrew, Bible, c. 10th century B.C.)

From THE FIRST BOOK OF SAMUEL "After the Shamans"

---

now Samuel was dead   all of Israel did the rites for him   & buried him in Ramah   his own city   & Saul had put away the ones that spoke with ghosts   the shamans   he sent them from the country

& the Philistines all came together   camped in Shunem   Saul & Israel together in Gilboa

& when Saul saw the army   of the Philistines   he was afraid   his heart was trembling

when he called to Yahveh   Yahveh would not answer   not by dreams   & not by oracles   & not by seers

then Saul told his servants   *find me a woman who can speak with ghosts that I can go to   make her sound her shaman bag   can speak through her*   his servants said   *well yes   there is a woman   mistress of the shaman bag   at Endor*

& Saul disguised himself   he changed his clothes   he went   & two men went with him   at night   they came to where she was Saul said to her   *show me divinings   sound your bag   raise up for me the one I name* the woman said to him   *well yes*   *you know what Saul has done*   *you know he banished those who speak with ghosts*   *the shamans*   *yes*   she said   *why must you lay a trap for me cause me to die*

Saul swore to her by Yahveh   *as sure as Yahveh lives no one will punish you for this thing*

then the woman said   *who should I bring you*   & he said   *bring up Samuel*

& when the woman saw Samuel she cried   her voice was loud   she spoke to Saul   she said   WHY HAVE YOU TRICKED ME YOU ARE SAUL

he said to her   the king   *don't be afraid what did you see*   the woman told him   *I saw gods ascending from the earth*   *saw elohim*

he said to her   *what form is he*   she said   *an old man comes up covered with a mantle*

& Saul perceived that it was Samuel   Saul stooped   his face was to the ground   he bowed himself

J.R.

COMMENTARY

(1) "Beforetime in Israel, when a man went to inquire of God, thus he spake, Come, & let us go to the seer: for he that is now called a Prophet was beforetime called a Seer." (I Samuel 9.9.)

(2) "Then the Lord put forth his hand & touched my mouth. And the Lord said unto me, Behold, I have put my words in thy mouth." (Jeremiah 1.9.)

(3) "Thou shalt not suffer a shaman to live." (Exodus 22.18.)

Amos the Prophet (Hebrew, Bible, 8th century B.C.)
A VISION IN THE VOICE OF YAHVEH

The Lord God has spoken;
who can but prophesy?
Amos 3.8

this is what Yahveh Adonai
showed me:
a basket of summer fruit

asked me: Amos what is this?
I said: a summer basket
he said: a summary for Israel
my people
never will I let it pass

but they will squawk their palace songs
that day
I say it Yahveh Adonai
there will be bodies everywhere
& silence

listen: you who suck
life from the poor man
drive him from his work

you say: when will the new moon pass
so we can sell grain?
when will the sabbath end
so we can show our wheat?
you weigh their baskets light
weigh your coins heavy
you cheaters with lying scales

you buy the poor for money
paupers for a pair of shoes
sell chaff for grain

God swears it by the pride of Jacob:
will I always be
forgetting?

will the earth shake some day —
all alive on her lament?
she'll rise up like a river
wholly
flooding drowning
like the Nile

that day the word of Yahveh Adonai
says:
I will make the sun turn back
at noon
earth will grow dark in daylight

will turn your feasts to mourning
songs to howls
wrap everybody's laps in sackcloth
everybody's head be shaved
be bald
will make it like grieving
for an only child

a bitter day to end it
days are coming
— says the word of Yahveh Adonai —
a famine in the land
will be no hungering for bread or water
but for Yahveh's words

J.R. / H.L.

COMMENTARY

(1) Arising at a time of invasions & internal conflicts, the work of the prophets
marked a shift in *poesis* toward new extremes: the delineation of moral pain, in which
the poet (prophet) stands as alienated conscience, accuser of his race. However the
words might seem in later, written form, as speech they struck against the going, still
repressive institutions of the state. The discourse that resulted, a late & particular

development of the prophetic frenzy, was devastating: a discovery of "history as nightmare" (Heschel) & of a "moral madness" in the face of human cruelty, which cast the prophet in the role of rebel but also led, one fears, to the creation of a new, cruel monster in turn – as in the Yahvists' push to eradicate their own predecessors & contemporaries among the shamans & the prophets of Baal, etc. What is evident too is a gradual movement from vision to voice, from "seers" to "hearers" & "speakers"; thus, as Blake wrote of Isaiah & Ezekiel: "The voice of Honest Indignation is the voice of God." The breakthrough is like a controlled paranoia in which "even a minor injustice assumes cosmic proportions." Writes an editor of the *Encyclopedia Judaica:* "The parallel to 'prophet' is 'madman' (*meshugga*)," a resemblance mentioned in the Bible & not unheard of in the poetics of our own time, etc.

(2) "Who could bear living in a state of disgust day & night? The conscience builds its confines, is subject to fatigue, longs for comfort, lulling, soothing. Yet those who are hurt, and He Who inhabits eternity, neither slumber nor sleep. . . . The prophet is human, yet he employs notes one octave too high for our ears. He experiences moments that defy our understanding. He is neither 'a singing saint' nor a 'moralizing poet,' but an assaulter of the mind." (Abraham J. Heschel, *The Prophets*, pages 9 – 10.)

Says prophet Jeremiah: "There is something in my heart like a burning fire / Shut up in my bones / & I am weary with holding it in / & I cannot" (20.9). And Menahem Mendel of Kotsk, a Hasidic master of the 19th century: "When a man has a reason to scream, & cannot though he wants to – he has achieved the greatest scream."

(Hebrew, 6th century B.C.)

PSALM 137   "Exile"

> *How can we sing King Alpha song*
> *In a strange land*

We sat & cried along Babylon rivers
remembering Zion.

We hung up our harps on Babylon trees
when our captors asked us for songs
when they mocked us calling for a happy tune:

"Sing us one of those Zion songs!"

If I forgot you Jerusalem
my right hand would wither
my tongue would stick to the roof of my mouth
if I didn't remember you
if I couldn't start up a tune with:
"Jerusalem ... "

YaHVeH recall the Edomites
Jerusalem's day   when they said:
"Strip her   Strip her bottom bare!"

Now   thief Babylon   (a song for you):

"Happy He'll be to pay you
    the reward you've rewarded us
Happy He'll be to snatch your babies
    and smash them against a rock!"

H.L.

COMMENTARY

Translation from the Hebrew text: this one a virtual song-of-protest made *in situ*
at the time of the Babylon "captivity." Lenowitz's epigraph is from a Jamaican reg-
gae (Rastafarian) version by B. Dowe & F. McNaughton, reflecting "another
movement-in-exile in which the leaders are singers" (H. Lenowitz). The reader
can also compare the refusal to sing with, e.g., the Acoma Indian: "long ago her
mother / had to sing this song and so / she had to grind along with it / the corn
people have a song too / it is very good / I refuse to tell it." (Translation by A.
Schwerner.)

(Hebrew, Bible, c. 9th century B.C.)

E L I J A H & T H E P R I E S T S O F B A A L   "In a Time of Famine"

vayehi
many days
the words of YaHVeH to Elijah
in the 3rd year (saying)
G O
let Ahab see you
I will truly bring down rain upon
Earth's face

      . . . .

vayehi
the moment Ahab saw Elijah
Ahab said
are Y O U the troublemaker
here in Israel

he said
I made no trouble here
in Israel
it's Y O U your kinsmen
Y O U left the rule of YaHVeH
Y O U pursued the Baals

now send now gather all of Israel
at the mountain called G O D ' S V I N E Y A R D
450 of Baal's prophets
400 of Ashera's
those who eat with Jezebel

      . . . .

vayehi
Elijah told the people
I remain
I stand as YaHVeH's prophet

I alone
Baal's prophets are 450 men

(he said) that they will give us
two young bulls
that they can choose the one bull for themselves
& cut it slice it in pieces put it on the branches
BUT SET NO FIRE TO IT
& I will do one bull will put it on the branches but SET NO FIRE TO IT

& you will call in the name of your elohim
& I will call in the name of YaHVeH
& the elohim that answers with fire is THE ELOHIM

(then everyone answered & said
that it was good)

& Elijah to Baal's prophets
CHOOSE ONE BULL & GO FIRST FOR YOU ARE MANY
& shout in the name of your elohim
BUT SET NO FIRE TO IT

& they did they took the bull he gave them they did it up they shouted in
    Baal's name
from morning until noon they shouted saying
ANSWER US O BAAL
(no voice no answerer they leaped over the slaughter-place he made for
    them)

vayehi
at noon Elijah minced beside them
(said)
SHOUT LOUDER LOUDER maybe your elohim is speaking maybe
    traveling 's on a journey maybe sleeping MAYBE WAKE HIM UP
& they shouted LOUDER LOUDER
they slashed themselves the way they do it with swords & spears
letting the blood flow over them

vayehi
when noon was passing
they still prophesied
until the offering of the seed

but got no voice
no answer
no one listening

then Elijah spoke to all the people
COME AROUND ME
all the people came around him
(he was healing YaHVeH's broken altar)

took 12 stones
(the number of the tribes
of Jacob's sons
YaHVeH's words had come to
told him
ISRAEL WILL BE YOUR NAME)

Elijah built an altar
out of stones
in YaHVeH's name & dug
a trench (2 troughs of seed
in width) around it

he spread out the branches
cut the bull in pieces
put it on the branches (saying)
FILL UP 4 JUGS WITH WATER
POUR WATER ON THE FIRE OFFERING
& ON THE BRANCHES

he said it twice
they twice
then thrice
they said it thrice

(water was then
around the altar
also he filled the trench
with water)

vayehi
the time of *minḥa*
of the offering of the seed

Elijah PROPHET came up close
& said

YAH ELOHIM
(of Abraham Isaac Israel)
today
let them find out that you
are ELOHIM are GOD in Israel
& I your slave
whose words
only were YOUR words

YAHVeH answer
answer me
this people then will know
YOU YAHVEH ARE THE ELOHIM
YOU WHO HAVE TURNED THEM UPSIDE DOWN

& Fire-of-YaHVeH fell
it fell devoured
the burnt offering
the branches
the stones & dust
licked up the water in the trench

the people saw it
fell down on their faces
saying
YAHVEH IS THE EL
YAHVEH IS THE ELOHIM

Elijah said to them
NOW GRAB HOLD OF BAAL'S PROPHETS
(let none of them escape)
& they grabbed hold of them
Elijah brought them down to Kishon Brook
& slaughtered them

he said to Ahab
GET UP & EAT & DRINK
THERE IS A SOUND OF HEAVY RAIN
(so Ahab went to eat & drink)

Elijah climbed up to the top of Carmel
crouched down on the earth
he put his face between his knees
& told his boy   GO UP NOW
look out towards the sea

(went up & looked
he said) not even a small trace
he told him
do it 7 times

vayehi
the 7th time
he said
a little cloud there
like a man's hand
on the sea

he said
move on now say to Ahab
HITCH IT UP
COME DOWN
THE RAIN WON'T STOP YOU

vayehi
the sky had darkened up
with clouds & wind

vayehi
a big rain
Ahab riding in the rain
towards Jezreel
the place they call
"god's seeding"

J.R. / H.L.

COMMENTARY

(1) "& the Children of Israel did what was wrong   in Yahveh's eyes   they served the Baals   the Ashtoreths   the gods of Syria   the gods of Sidon   the gods of Moab   the gods of Ammon's sons   the gods of the Philistines   they turned from Yahveh   they abandon Yahveh" (Judges 10.6.)

(2) Thus: the struggle between Yahveh & the (so-called) "strange gods" runs from here throughout the Bible. But the question persists, if the intrusions are merely foreign (Baal's prophets, above, are more than likely Jews) or are variants in fact of the Hebrew-Jewish vision in conflict with each other. Writes Raphael Patai: "Let us here stress the fact that in addition to 'official' Judaism – that crystallization of the religion which represented the consensus of most of the religious leaders of a certain time and place – Judaism has always comprised heterodox variants as well. . . . There can be no doubt that down to the very end of the Hebrew monarchy the worship of old Canaanite gods was an integral part of the religion of the Hebrews. . . . The reason is not far to seek. The image of Yahweh, in the eyes of the common people, did not differ greatly from that of Baal or other Canaanite male gods. Often it would have been difficult to determine whether a certain cult was legitimately Yahwistic, heretically Yahwistic, or unequivocally pagan. The worship of Yahweh thus easily merged into, complemented or supplanted that of the Canaanite male gods." (*The Hebrew Goddess,* pages 20, 25.)

Even more so, the persistence of the goddesses: Ashera, Anat, Ashtoreth, as bride of God (*El*) & Queen of Heaven.

(3) For more on Jewish rain-making – another survival of shamanic traditions, etc. – see above, page 67, below, page 247.

(Ugaritic, c. 1400 B.C.)

From A POEM ABOUT ASHERA:
HOW SHE GOES TO BULL GOD EL
TO SEEK A HOUSE FOR BAAL HER SON

                              So Ashera sets out
                              toward El
at the Flowing of the Two Rivers,
near the Fountain of the Two Deeps.
                              She arrives at the Field of El.
She walks onto the platform
of the KING
the FATHER OF YEARS.
She bends, then
falls.
She bows.
                              She pays homage to him.

                              As soon as El
                              discovers her,
                              his narrowed lips part,
                              and he laughs.

                              He puts his feet up
                              on a footstool.

                              He twiddles his thumbs.

                              He raises his voice
                              and calls,
"What has Lady Ashera of the Sea
come for?
What has the Queen of the Gods
come for?

You must be hungry?
You're surely thirsty?

Have something to eat
or drink.
There is food on the tables,
drink in the goblets,
wine in a golden cup,
trees' blood,
if the affection of KING EL
stirs you,
if the BULL's love
moves you."

                           Lady Ashera of the Sea says,

"EL
your word is wise,
eternal with wisdom:
happiness and your word are one.
Our King is
Almighty Baal,
our Judge,
and there is none over him.
So by our cry
fill his jug,
fill his cup
as we cry to you.

He calls loudly
to BULL EL
his father,
EL his KING

                         who made him.

He calls to Ashera
and her sons,
to the goddess
and her mass of offspring,

'Look, there is
no house for Baal
as the Gods have,
and no court
as Ashera's sons have.

EL's home is a shelter
for his son:

the home of Lady Ashera of the Sea
is a home

> for the untouched brides:
> Pidraya's home,
> the daughter of Light,
> Talaya's home,
> the daughter of Rain,
> the home of Artsaya
> daughter of Y'bdr.'"

> And EL of the GENTLE
> HEART says,

"Am I to be an agent of Ashera,
to carry hods?

If Ashera will be a slave
making bricks
a house will be built
for Baal
as the other Gods have,
with a courtyard
fit for a son of Ashera."

> And Lady Ashera of the Sea says,

"Lord of the Gods in wisdom,
the grey of your beard has surely taught you something."

H.L.

COMMENTARY

"The Goddess Asherah was worshipped in Israel from the days of the first settle-
ment in Canaan, the Hebrews having taken over the cult of the great mother god-
dess from the Canaanites.... It appears that of the 370 years during which the
Solomonic Temple stood in Jerusalem, for no less than 236 years ... the statue of
Asherah was present in the Temple and her worship was a part of the legitimate re-
ligion approved and led by the king, the court and the priesthood, and opposed only
by a few prophetic voices crying out against it at relatively long intervals.... One
cannot belittle the emotional gratification with which she must have rewarded her
servants who saw in her the loving, motherly consort of Yahweh-Baal, and for
whom she was the great mother-goddess, giver of fertility, that greatest of all bless-
ings." (Raphael Patai, *The Hebrew Goddess*, pages 42, 50, 52.)

*o Ephraim you have played the harlot —
Israel is defiled*

(Hosea 5.3.)

(Hebrew, medieval)

From THE ALPHABET OF BEN SIRA   "The Birth"

As it is written HE DOETH GREAT THINGS PAST FINDING
OUT, YEA, MARVELOUS THINGS WITHOUT NUMBER
(Job 9.10.)

Now see how great are the deeds of the Holy One Be Blest for if it says
HE DOETH GREAT THINGS PAST FINDING OUT why
should it say MARVELOUS THINGS WITHOUT NUMBER &
if it says MARVELOUS THINGS WITHOUT NUMBER why
should it say HE DOETH GREAT THINGS PAST FINDING
OUT? What does it mean? And so our wise men may their memory be
blest explained: HE DOETH GREAT THINGS PAST FIND-
ING OUT why this pertains to all the works of creation & MARVEL-
OUS THINGS WITHOUT NUMBER why this pertains to those
three born without their mothers lying with a man. And those three were
Ben Sira & Rav Papa & Rabbi Zira: all of them total saints & all great wise
men.

And this is what they say about them. First about Rav Papa & Rabbi Zira:
that in all their lives they never carried on an idle conversation: that they
never slept in the study house no not even for a cat nap: that no man ever got
down to the study house before them nor ever found them sitting quietly
but rather sitting studying: that no day passed but that they made it holy &
never did they gossip about friends & never did they profit by a friend's
misfortune never did friends curse them on their death beds & never did
they look upon a crucifix & never took a bribe: for they were like a sturdy
mast fulfilling what was written LEADING THOSE WHO LOVE
ME & FILLING UP THEIR TREASURES. (Proverbs 8.21.)
And how did it happen that their mothers should have given birth without a
husband? Here they say: one time they went down to the bath house & a
seed of Israel went up into their holes & they were pregnant & they gave
birth but the children never knew who was their father.

But Ben Sira did know who his father was & how his mother gave birth without a man to do the man's thing. This is what they say about her: she was the daughter of the prophet Jeremiah & once when Jeremiah went to the bath house he spied some rough trade from the tribe of Ephraim all of whom were beating out their own seed making waste of it but the whole tribe of Ephraim in that generation was full of such as these as written: HE HAS DONE THE EVIL THING IN GOD'S EYE. And when Jeremiah saw them he began to call them down & they immediately moved in on him they said: WHY SHOULD YOU CALL US DOWN LIKE THAT? LONG LIVE THE WAY OF BEERSHEBA. And they said: WE WON'T LET YOU GO FROM HERE UN-TIL YOU DO IT JUST LIKE US. He said: JUST LET ME BE I SWEAR TO YOU I'LL KEEP IT SECRET. But they said back to him: DIDN'T ZEDEKIAH SEE NEBUCHADNEZZAR EAT A LIVING RABBIT & DIDN'T HE SWEAR TO HIM BY GOD'S DECREE HE'D KEEP IT SECRET & DIDN'T HE THEN GO & BREAK HIS OATH? AND YOU WOULD TOO. BUT NOW IF YOU JUST DO LIKE US WE'LL LET YOU GO BUT IF YOU DON'T WE'LL SODOMIZE YOU LIKE OUR FATHERS DID IT IN THEIR WEIRD RELI-GIONS & IF THEY DID THAT MUCH IN THEIR WEIRD RELIGIONS WE'LL DO IT EVEN MORE ON YOU. He was so frightened then so fearful that he did it right off just as they had said but then as soon as he had gotten out of there he cursed his day the way it's written CURSED BE THE DAY WHEN I WAS BORN (Jere-miah 20.12) & went off & fasted 248 fasts one for each part of a man's body. But a drop of this very saint remained until the daughter of this very saint went to the bath house & it got into her hole & after seven months she bore a son equipped with teeth & talking. Once she gave birth she felt ashamed: people she felt would think that she had come to it by whoring. But then the child opened his mouth he said to his mother: WHY DO YOU FEEL ASHAMED FOR PEOPLE? Then he told her: I AM SIRA'S SON. She said to him: WHO IS THIS SIRA? He told her: JERE-MIAH. And she asked: WHY CALL HIM SIRA? He said: BE-CAUSE HE IS A SIRE ABOVE ALL SIRES A PRINCE ABOVE ALL PRINCES: IT IS HE WILL GIVE HIS NAME TO EVERY PRINCE & KING BECAUSE WHEN YOU COUNT UP SIRA & JEREMIAH BY GEMATRIA THEY COME OUT EQUAL. Then she said to him: MY SON SHOULDN'T YOU HAVE BETTER SAID I AM A SON OF JEREMIAH? He said to her: I WOULD HAVE SAID IT BUT THE THOUGHT WAS TOO REPUGNANT SAYING

THAT JEREMIAH COVERED HIS OWN DAUGHTER. She said to him: MY SON ISN'T THERE A PROVERB THAT WHAT HAS BEEN IS WHAT WILL BE? (Ecclesiastes 1.9.) YET WHO EVER SAW A DAUGHTER PREGNANT FROM HER FATHER? He said to her: O MOTHER NOTHING IS NEW UNDER THE SUN: AS LOT WAS EVERY INCH A SAINT SO WAS MY FATHER & AS WHAT WAS DONE TO LOT WAS DONE BY FORCE SO WAS IT TO MY FATHER. She said to him: YOU FRIGHTEN ME. HOW DO YOU KNOW THESE THINGS? He said to her: DO NOT BE FRIGHTENED BY ME BECAUSE NOTHING IS NEW UNDER THE SUN. LOOK AT MY FATHER JEREMIAH THIS IS WHAT HE DID TOO WHEN HIS OWN MOTHER BENT TO HEAR HIM YES HE OPENED UP HIS MOUTH HE CALLED HIS FATHER FROM THE BELLY OF HIS MOTHER & SAID I won't come out until they tell me what my name is. THEN HIS FATHER OPENED HIS MOUTH HE SAID: Get out your name is Abraham. HE SAID: That's not my name. HE SAID TO HIM: Your name is Isaac Jacob IN THAT ORDER NAMING ALL THE TRIBES & ALL THE FIGURES OF THAT GENERATION BUT HE SAID That's not my name. UNTIL ELIJAH MAY HIS MEMORY BE BLEST PASSED BY HE SAID: Your name will be called Jeremiah which is Yirmiyahu which is God Will Lift for in your days the Holy One Be Blest will raise an enemy & he will lift his hand against Jerusalem. HE SAID TO HIM: That really is my name & you because you said my name my name will be like yours Elijah which is Eliyahu I will take the Yahu from it for my name of Yirmiyahu which is Jeremiah. AND JUST AS HE CAME OUT SPEAKING I CAME OUT SPEAKING JUST AS HE CAME OUT PROPHESYING FROM THE BELLY OF HIS MOTHER AS THE SAYING GOES: Before I made you in the belly I did know you (Jeremiah 1.5) SO I CAME OUT PROPHESYING. AS HE CAME OUT FROM THE BELLY OF HIS MOTHER WITH A NAME SO I CAME OUT FROM THE BELLY OF MY MOTHER WITH MY NAME. AS HE MADE A BOOK AROUND THE "ALFA-BETA" SO I WILL MAKE A BOOK AROUND THE "ALFA-BETA." SO DON'T BE FRIGHTENED BY MY WORDS. She said to him: MY SON DON'T BRAG THE EVIL EYE MAY OVERPOWER YOU. He said to her: THE EVIL EYE WOULD HAVE NO CAUSE TO OVERPOWER ME SO NOW DON'T GO ON SPEAKING ABOUT ME BECAUSE I'M ONLY

DOING WHAT MY FATHER DID. THERE IS A SAYING
ABOUT ME THAT AS A SHEEP FOLLOWS A SHEEP A
SON'S DEEDS FOLLOW ON HIS FATHER'S. (Talmud:
Ketubot.) She said to him: MY SON WHY WOULD YOU STOP
MY SPEAKING? He said to her: BECAUSE YOU KNOW
THAT I'M HUNGRY BUT HAVEN'T GIVEN ME TO EAT.
She said: HERE ARE MY BREASTS FOR YOU FOR EAT-
ING & FOR DRINKING. He said: NO NO I DO NOT CRAVE
YOUR BREASTS GO INSTEAD & SIFT FLOUR FIND A
CHICKEN KNEAD FRESH BREAD GET MEAT & OIL &
OLD WINE & COME EAT WITH ME. She said to him: HOW
CAN I BUY THESE THINGS? He said to her: MAKE
CLOTHES & SELL THEM SO THE VERSE WILL BE
FULFILLED THROUGH YOU: a sheet she made & sold (Proverbs
31.24) & IF YOU NOURISH ME FOR A YEAR THE OTHER
VERSES WILL BE FULFILLED THROUGH YOU: many a
valiant daughter but you above them all. (Proverbs 31.29.)

So she began to make clothes & sell them & she brought him bread &
meat oil & wine & she nourished him a year.

J.R. / H.L.

COMMENTARY

(1) The actual Ben Sira, author of Ecclesiasticus (The Wisdom of Ben Sira), goes
back to the 2nd century B.C.; the connection with the earlier Jeremiah relates to the
numerical equivalence of their names, etc. The *Alphabet* itself is a much later
(medieval) work: a series of epigrams & stories arranged alphabetically. Satirical,
pornographic, "heretical" in its thrusts "not only," as here, "[at] Jeremiah . . . & all
the institutions of established religion . . . but God . . . as well." (Joseph Dan, in
Encyclopedia Judaica, volume 4, page 549.)

(2) "The world like Great Sodom lies under Love
and knows not the hand of the Lord that moves"

– Robert Duncan

Meshullam the Great ben Kalonymos (Hebrew, 10th century)

A POEM FOR THE HIGH PRIEST, SUNG THERE-
AFTER ON THE DAY OF THE KIPPURIM,
AS HE WAS CELEBRATED ALSO
IN "THE WISDOM OF BEN SIRA"

like a tent
    stretched tight
            around the ones who live
                            above
was the appearance of the priest

like lightning
        breaking from
                the brightness of
                        his beasts
was the appearance of the priest

like knots
    the knotting at
            the four
            extremities
was the appearance of the priest

like the rainbow's
            image
            in middle of
                the cloud
was the appearance of the priest

like the splendor
        which
            he wrapped
            o Rock
                    around his fashionings
was the appearance of the priest

like a rose
    set in
        the middle of
            the garden
                of sweet love
was the appearance of the priest

like a headband
    set upon
        the forehead
            of a king
was the appearance of the priest

like the love
    that settled on
        the bridegroom's
            face
was the appearance of the priest

like the clear light
    set within
        his turban's
            light
was the appearance of the priest

like the man who sits
    in secret
        to entreat
        a king
was the appearance of the priest

like the star
    called brightness
        at the limits of
            the east
was the appearance of the priest

J.R.

COMMENTARY

(1) "There is a teaching in the name of Rabbi Yose, saying: When the priest spreads forth his hands it is forbidden to look at them, for the reason that the Shekinah is hovering over his hands. . . . At that moment there is a whisper followed by silence throughout the universe. So when a king is about to join his queen, all his attendants are agog and a whisper runs through them: Behold, the King is about to meet his Matrona." (*Zohar* 3.147a, 146a.)

(2) "We are told that a priest not beloved by the people ought not to take part in blessing the people. On one occasion, when a priest went up and spread forth his hands, before he completed the blessing he turned into a heap of bones. This happened to him because there was no love between him and the people." (*Zohar* 3.147b.)

(Syriac, c. 3rd century A.D.)

From THE ACTS OF SAINT JOHN

"The Round Dance of Jesus"

     "A praise poem
"we sing now
"will go to meet what is to come
& had us form a circle
we stood in with folded hands
himself was in the middle
(said) You answer
Amen
then started singing
praises saying
"Praises Father
circling & we answered him
Amen (said)
Praises Word (said)
Praises Grace
Amen (said)

Praises   Spirit   (said)
Praises   Holy Holy   (said)
O thee transfiguration   (said)
Amen   (said)
Thank you   Sunshine   Light
no darkness   (said)
"I will inform you now
"the reason for this thanks
(then said)
I save
& will be saved
Amen
I free
& will be freed
Amen
I hurt
& will be hurt
Amen
Am born
& will give birth
Amen
I feed
& will be food
Amen
I hear
& will be heard
Amen
I will be known
all knowing mind
Amen
I will be washed
& I will wash
Amen
all Grace Sweet Mind the Dance is round
I blow the pipe for
all are in the Round Dance
I will pipe
all dance along
Amen
I will moan low
all beat your breasts

Amen
the One & Only Eight
plays up for us
Amen
Old Number Twelve
stomps up above
Amen
the Universe controls
the dancer
Amen
whoever isn't dancing
's in the dark
Amen
I will go
& I will stay
Amen
I will dress thee
& I will dress
Amen
I will be Oned
& I will One
Amen
I have no house
& I have houses
Amen
I have no place
& I have places
Amen
I have no temple
& I have temples
Amen
I am a lamp to thee
who see me
Amen
I am a mirror to thee
who view me
Amen
I am a door to thee
who come thru me
Amen
I am a way to thee
wayfarer

Amen   (said)
"Follow
"my Round Dance
"& see yourself in me
"the Speaker
"& seeing what I speak
"keep silent on
"my mysteries
"or dancing think of what
"I do
"make yours the suffering of a man
"that I will suffer
"yet powerless to understand your suffering
"without a word
"the Father sent language thru me
"the sufferer you saw
"& saw me suffering
"you grew restless
"shaken
"you were moved toward wisdom
"lean on me
"I am a pillow
"who am I?
"you only will know me
"when I'm gone –
"but am not he for whom
"I am now taken –
"will know it when you reach it
"& knowing suffering will know
"how not to suffer
"I am your god
"not the betrayer's
"will harmonize the Sweet Soul with my own
"the Word of Wisdom speaks in me
"says
"Praises   Father
& we answered him
Amen   (said)
Praises   Word   (said)
Praises   Grace
Amen   (said)
Praises   Spirit   (said)

Praises   Holy Holy   (said)
"& if thou wouldst understand that which is me
"know this   all that I have said I have uttered
"playfully   & I was by no means ashamed of it
"I danced
"& when you dance in understanding
"understand & say
"Amen

J.R.

COMMENTARY

The figure of Jesus emerges, dark & shining in the pattern of other Jewish messiahs from then to present, & enters history. With him he carries the older metaphors of transformation: *I will make you a god to Pharaoh . . . the Patriarchs are the Merkaba . . . Israel the first born, logos . . . son of God* – working the change not only on himself but on his fellow Jews as well. For it is from this point on that *we* are drawn into the paranoia of the *other:* are transformed ("betrayers," "murderers") & locked into a system of thought, of action & response, which dominates & robs us of control over our lives.

The Jews, by Jesus' time, had already moved into the world outside Judaea. With the wars of that first century the land itself was taken from them – irrevocably in the Christian triumph that would follow. The visible Jewish response was further to literalize the Torah, to bring all into the domain of the written: to replace the broken temple with the study-house, the rites of sacrifice with those of prayers & exegesis ("exiled in the word"). But beneath that surface other forces stirred: a secret transmission or kabbala that kept alive a poetics of liberation & an anger that produced further messiahs, further failed revolutionaries & mystics, fantasies of escape from exile, & a continuing dream of freedom in a world in which "a fence was built around the Law."

For the later messiahs Jesus remained a covert model. Multiphasic from the start, he appeared in a variety of forms to the early Jewish Christians, including the dancer-of-the-mysteries & playful trickster in the gnostic Acts of Saint John. Thus he was himself a creature of the *nous poetikos* (creative mind) that would proliferate his image through the world. But the source of that image was still Jewish: prophetic & visionary & sharing that other side of the Jewish psyche that Gershom Scholem describes for Sabbatai Zevi, messiah of a later age: "[a movement] with its doctrine so profoundly shocking to the Jewish conception of things that the violation of the Torah could become its true fulfillment . . . [yet] a dialectical outgrowth of the belief in [his] Messiahship. . . . Not only . . . a single continuous development which retained its identity in the eyes of its adherents regardless of whether they themselves remained Jews or not, but also, paradoxical though it may seem, a specifically *Jewish* phenomenon. . . . " (From *The Messianic Idea in Judaism,* page 84.)

For more on the "heretical" messiahs, etc., see below, page 126.

(Hebrew, traditional)

A POEM FOR BAR YOḤAI

o you Bar Yoḥai
             you in oil
     be happy
oil joy from
             your friends
o you Bar Yoḥai
     holy
             oiling you with oil
you oiled
     & measured holy
             you hold up
a leaf from Holy Crown
     held on your head
             your beauty
o you Bar Yoḥai
     your good home
             you homed in
the day you ran
     you roamed
             Hole of the Rocks
you hid in
     gave you glory
             halos for your head
o you Bar Yoḥai
     circle of whose trees surround
             lore of Adonai
study
     wondrous light
             o hearthlight
glows for you
     your teachers
             teach you
o you Bar Yoḥai
     o you flew
             you in the applefield

you drew flowers
          odors
                    o secrets of
the Torah
          buds & branches
                    you for whom we speak
o you Bar Yoḥai
          wore your power
                    in faith's war
fire
          at its gates
                    pulled sword
from sheath
          you drew against
                    your enemies
o you Bar Yoḥai
          where the stones were
                    marble
you were there
          before the lion
                    you who saw the bear's
crown jewel
          (saw
                    but who saw you?)
o you Bar Yoḥai
          in holiest of
                    holies
green line
          months made months
                    the seven sabbaths
secrets of the fifty
          linked the links of *shin*
                    your links
o you Bar Yoḥai
          wisdom's ancient *yod*
                    you saw
into his glory
          32-fold path
                    o onset of high offerings

a cherub enters
>   oiled & shining in
>>   your light
o you Bar Yoḥai
>   wondrous light
>>   o high above you
frightened
>   past all sight
>>   & hidden
call it nothing
>   call it sleep
>>   eyes cannot see

J.R. / H.L.

COMMENTARY

A pupil of Akiba's (mid-2nd century A.D.), Simeon bar Yoḥai came to be identified with the ecstatic side of *poesis,* itself not separated from the developing Jewish otherness, resistance. Sentenced to death for talk against the Roman state during Bar Kokhba's war (circa 132 A.D.), he hid with his son Eleazar in a cave for twelve years; was credited much later as "author" of the *Zohar.* The anniversary of his death has been celebrated since at least the 16th century as a festival (*hilula*) in the village of Meron in Israel; marked by a night-long series of potlatch-like fire events (in which money, costly garments, the first-cut locks of three-year-old boys, etc., are thrown into a great fire), accompanied by singing & ecstatic dances, healing rites & fire-handling. Bar Yoḥai's hymn (the *ashrekha*) is sung as a series of ten strophes corresponding to the ten *sefirot,* & new songs in Hebrew & Arabic are still composed for the event.

(Hebrew / Aramaic, written c. 499 A.D.)

THE GREAT LAMENT

for the Rabbis

The columns of Caesarea ran with tears, roof gutters ran with blood, stars
    were visible in the daytime
All cedars were uprooted
All trees were uprooted
Fiery stones fell from heaven
All images were effaced and were used as stone pillars
All statues of humans were torn out of position
Seventy houses were broken into by thieves at Tiberias
Hail stones fell from heaven
The rocks of the Euphrates kissed each other
The rocks of the Tigris kissed each other
The palms were laden with thorns

THE END OF "A BOOK OF BEARDS"

A Book of the Wars of Yahveh

Rochelle Owens (b. 1936)

From I AM THE BABE OF JOSEPH STALIN'S
DAUGHTER

DIN
who am i floating
above cows
YAHOEL AM I
whiter than   white
animal skins   unblemished
lambs.   my blood
so red & light salty
Isaac Resnikoff
the pious scribe
studies my .word.
it is as if sacred white scrolls

"A Book of the Wars of Yahveh" is also the "Book of the Exile": an assemblage of voices in anger & pain, rebellion & madness, hatred of other & of self. Here "history" is truly "nightmare" (see page 99, above), & the face God shows is that of *D I N* or J U D G M E N T. The book sketches a record of *poesis* (vision, voice) as the struggle for human survival in a world of mind-forged manacles & racial bondage. It moves from the political & religious upheavals under the Romans (Jesus & other "messiahs," destruction of Temple & city, Shekinah's withdrawal from same into years of sterility) to new rebellions, enforced diaspora, medieval visions of heaven & hell, dreams of new zions, messiahs & mystics who work within a web of cruelty & persecution, bending the Law to their visions or striking against it toward a growing concern with liberation: mystical, secular, radical, zionist, subterranean, criminal, etc. The terror, if not the triumph, is both Jewish & human: the disasters of a civilization that moves along the road to Auschwitz, Hiroshima. (The [re]creation of the Jewish "state" – & of a second people's exile & resistance – is the current moment in the work's chronology.) The events, as in "A Book of Beards," are roughly chronological – the writings about those events from various times & places. The participants throughout are Jews, not saints.

```
encase my holy legs          Rising I Rise
        over this peculiar
                continent
                        I float
    above cities    singing glory glory
I am living prayer &
                THEY give me their
        .love.
                I Am That I Am
        DIVINE STERNNESS
                *

                J U D G M E N T
        DIN
```

Jesus ben Hananiah (Hebrew / Aramaic, 1st century A.D.)

THE PROPHECY OF JESUS BEN HANANIAH

---

a voice from the sunrise
a voice from the sunset
a voice from the 4 winds:

cry for Jerusalem & the temple
cry for the bridegroom & the bride
cry for all of their people

COMMENTARY

A 1st-century prophet & messiah, Jesus ben Hananaiah repeated this oracle for years prior to the city's fall & again at his death in the siege of Jerusalem. Other 1st-century "messiahs" included Jesus of Nazareth, Simon Magus, Judah the Galilean, the Pharisee Saddok, Theudas, Menahem ben Judah, & Simeon bar Giora; thereafter: Simeon bar Kokhba, Abu Isa, Yudqhan, Mushka, Ibn Aryeh, Solomon ha-Kohen, Moses Al-Dari, David Alroy, Abraham Abulafia, the Prophet of Avila, Hasdai Crescas, Asher Lemlein, David Reuveni, Solomon Molcho, Sabbatai Zevi, & Jacob Frank. The list of claimants, mystical & revolutionary by turns, is far from complete.

I

back then • the government of Israel was in a woman's hand a woman's hands whose name was Helen • in the temple stood the stone called Stone-That-Yah-Set-Up that had the letters of the Holy Name cut in • *who learns these letters can do anything* the wise ones thought • they were afraid the young ones if they learned them would destroy the world • the wise ones were afraid they bound two dogs of brass to the two iron pillars at the Gate of the Burnt Offerings (said) *whoever comes in here & learns the letters let the dogs howl at him then let the letters leave his mind* • well in comes Jesus • then he learned the letters wrote them on a parchment slit his thigh & laid the parchment in • he felt no pain • no pain the flesh closed up around it • going out the dogs bound to the pillars howled the letters left his mind • he went back to his house & with a knife he cut his flesh & lifted out the writing • how he learned the Name

2

rebellion growing • great division throughout Israel • then Jesus leaves for Upper Galilee • the wise ones come before the Queen they say *Our Lady this one is a sorcerer he leads the world to ruin* • well she sends her horsemen after him they find him stirring up the men of Galilee he says *I am the son of God* he says *it says so in your Torah* • well the horsemen try to take him but the men of Galilee resist • a war starts • Jesus tells them *you don't have to fight just trust the power of My Father In Heaven* • well the Galileans had been making birds from clay then Jesus spoke the letters of the Name & just like that they flapped their wings • right then the men fell down before him • then he tells them *bring a millstone* • so they roll it to the seashore where he speaks the letters sets it on the sea & just like sitting in a boat he's floating on the water • horsemen dazzled • Jesus says to them *you tell your lady tell her what you saw here* • then he makes the spirit lift him from the water & put him on dry land • when they go back to the Queen & tell her then she is amazed & trembling • she really is amazed

3

*then the Elders of Israel took a certain man whose name was Judas Iscariot &
brought him into the house of the holy of holies • & he learned the letters of the
Ineffable Name which were engraved on the foundation stone* : & he wrote them
on a small parchment slit his thigh & laid the parchment in • he felt no
pain just as Jesus had felt no pain before him • then when Jesus & his men
came in before the Queen & the wise ones she had told to be there Jesus
spoke up first he said *Of me the prophecy was made : dogs encompassed me about
I did not fear them* • then the wise ones came in with Judas they began
accusing him & he accusing them & saying to the Queen *of me King David
said : I will ascend to heaven* • *& he wrote : he shall receive me* (selah) • well
he raises up his hands like eagles' wings & takes off • everyone's amazed
they say *how can he fly there between the sky & earth* • the elders say to Judas
sound the letters & fly after him • then Judas does it just like that he flies into
the sky & everyone's amazed *how both of them can fly like eagles* • until
Iscariot grabs hold of him & flies up higher soars can't force him down to
earth • neither one can beat the other with the Name the Name shared
equally between them • but when Judas saw that this was so he played it
dirty yes he pissed on Jesus even buggered him until he got unclean &
down he fell to earth & Judas with him • well they weep about this on their
night they cry for what he did to him • & right away they seized him & they
said to Helen : *Let him be destroyed* they said : *Or let him say who beat him*
• & they put a coat over his head & banged on him with pomegranate
branches • well he didn't know a word to use against them • how they
knew the power of the Name had left him

J.R. / H.L.

COMMENTARY

Toldot Yeshu was a Jewish "life of Jesus," or counter-gospel, many versions of which
were compiled & written from the geonic period on, though obviously relying on
earlier sources. Similar magical abuses were attributed by the early Christians to
other messiahs like Simon Magus or to the Jews in general: "And what are the
wonders that he works?. . . . Sometimes he flies." (*The Clementine Homilies*, II.32.)
In Jewish folklore Jesus remains a "magician" or latterday (dark) shaman – as here,
with Judas, in a struggle of shamanic forces.

Yehuda ben Idi (Hebrew, 3rd / 4th century A.D.)

THE WITHDRAWAL OF THE SHEKINAH FROM HER HOME IN THE TEMPLE

after Yoḥanan bar Nappaḥa

from the ark cover she moved onto the Cherub
from the Cherub onto the other Cherub
from the second Cherub onto the threshold of the Temple
from the threshold into the court of the Priests
from the court onto the altar in the court
from the altar onto the roof of the Temple
from the roof onto the wall
from the wall into the city of Jerusalem
from the city onto the Mount of Olives
from the Mount of Olives into the desert

COMMENTARY

"A new chapter in the life of the Matronit [Shekinah as divine daughter & bride of God] opened when her bedchamber, the Temple of Jerusalem, was destroyed. Since her husband, the King, was wont to copulate with her only in the Temple, its destruction meant the sudden disruption of the intensely pursued love-relationship between the two. . . . The Matronit was banished from her holy abode and from the Land of Israel. . . . The King . . . lost stature and power, was no longer King, nor great, nor potent. . . . [Unable] to endure the misery of solitude, he let a slave-goddess take the place of his true queen . . . [:] none other than Lilith, [who] now assumed the rule over the Holy Land. . . . This act, more than anything else, caused the King to lose his honor." (R. Patai, *Hebrew Goddess,* pages 196 – 97.) But the exile of the Shekinah (= Israel) is also the "separation of the masculine and feminine principles in God" (G. Scholem): the exile of God from God, etc. The restoration may then be seen – in Blake's sense or in Reich's – as a "heightening of sensual pleasure," God & his Shekinah mating, says the *Zohar,* "face to face." (For more on the Shekinah, etc., see page 36, above.)

(Hebrew, traditional)

A CURSE & ANGRY POEM AGAINST THE NATIONS

this word is spoken at
the open door:
for the Prophet Eliahu

I

THE CURSE

pour out thy wrath upon the nations that do not know thee & upon the
kingdoms that call not upon thy name for they have beaten Jacob & laid
waste his dwelling: pour out thy wrath upon them : & may the kindling of
thine anger overtake them : pursue them with anger & destroy them from
under God's skies

2

THE POEM

not to us Adonai not to us
but to your name
be praises

for love of us
for truth's sake

why should the *goyim* say:
where is their god?

& our god in the skies

all that he wanted
done

their idols
gold & silver

workings of the hands
of man

whose mouths
are wordless

eyes are sightless

ears are deaf

nose dead to smell

hands without touch
feet without motion

can't utter sound
thru throats

like these be those
who made them

J.R.

Moses de Leon (Hebrew, c. 1240–1305)

From MIDRASH OF THE ABSENT   "Messiah"

---

the Garden has three walls all made of fire   an outer wall that holds the
righteous of the gentiles   a second wall that holds all those who wait
upon Messiah who see Messiah once a day   on Friday from the time
Israel begins its rest all the palaces inside the Garden shake   & the
inner palace is Messiah's & is called the Bird's Nest   & Messiah comes
out from there & the tsadikim come out with him   & Messiah wears
clothes of vengeance for the coming victory of Israel   & all come in with
him & he comes out there with the Fathers   then he stands there in
middle of the Garden   he stands where the pillar stands there in the
middle   & he grabs the 4 rings at the 4 corners of the Garden & lifts his

voice   the dome over the Garden vibrates & the 7 Angels called before
him say   CHOSEN ONE OF YAH BE STILL   FOR THE
TIME IS HERE WHEN THE EVIL KINGDOM WILL BE
TORN OUT FROM ITS PLACE   & they hear a voice out of the
synagogues & studyhouses a cry of power   AMEN MAY HIS
GREAT NAME BE BLEST FOREVER   then the Holy-One-
Be-Blest shakes all the domes & drops 2 tears into the Great Ocean   &
the tsadikim come back & Messiah comes back with them to the palace
called the Bird's Nest   in the Garden   on the side of the East Wind
        there is a palace hidden & shut tight   & this one is called the Palace
of the Glow   this one this palace built "like the pure substance of the
heavens"   from the walls around it letters burst & sparkle rising & de-
scending   flying up from one side coming to rest at the other
exchanging places but without confusion   & no one can stand beside
them for they do not stop their motion not even for a moment   & flowers
spun from the 4 colors of the glow spark toward the palace   on the
sabbath Messiah comes there with the Fathers   & the letters quiet
down the letters speak the letters sing a joyous song   but nobody knows
what it is
        & there inside that palace is an opening   & there behind the curtain
there are images of those killed at Lod   & images of the 10 killed by the
Kingdom   Messiah rises up & enters there & sees those images & lifts
his voice & bellows like a lion   & the whole Garden shakes & the
tsadikim shake   & the pillar in the middle of the Garden shakes up &
down   & 4 Angels of the Wheel are called & catch hold of the 4 rings &
the dome is spinning & a voice sounds from the heights   & the Holy-
One-Be-Blest lets 2 tears fall directly down   & the wheels come in to
the Messiah & all the Fathers come in through the opening in the Eastern
Gate inside that palace   & there they see the varying degrees of the
tsadikim killed at Lod & the 10 killed by the Kingdom   & all stand with
Messiah   & the wheels lift up & raise them to the King the King of
Kings the Holy-One-Be-Blest who swears that he will put on clothes of
vengeance he will execute his vengeance on the gentiles   for they say
"he will judge among the gentiles   he will fill the earth with
corpses"   & they come back to Messiah

J.R. / H.L.

Abraham Abulafia (Hebrew, 1240–c. 1291)

HOW HE WENT AS MESSIAH IN THE NAME OF ANGEL RAZIEL TO CONFRONT THE POPE

> Naḥmanides: *And so when the eskaton arrives   the messiah will*
> *come to the Pope   by command of the Name and will say   "Send*
> *out my people that they may serve me"   and then he will have come*
> (from an argument between Naḥmanides
> and Paolo Christiani   Barcelona, 1264)

This *Book of Witness* is the fourth book of Raziel's explanations . . . until
this year he had not composed a book which might be called "prophecy"
. . . and in that good year the Name awoke him to go to great Rome   He
commanded him in Barcelona   in the year "These" and five thousand
[1280] . . . in going he passed through Trani and was taken captive by
goyim   because of slanders Jews had laid against him   but a miracle
was done him   YHVH aided him   and he was delivered . . . went
through Capua . . . and in the month of Av came to Rome . . . and
determined to go before the Pope the day before Rosh Hashana   And
the Pope commanded his guards   while he was in Soriano   a certain
city a day's walk from Rome   that if Raziel should come there to speak
with him in the name of all Jewry   that they should take him immediate-
ly   and that he would not see him at all   but that they should take
him out of the city and burn him by fire   and there was the firewood
behind the city's inner wall   but this thing was announced to Raziel
      He paid no attention to the words of the speakers   but went away
by himself   and saw sights   and wrote them   and made this new
book   and called it the *Book of Witness*   it being a witness between
him and the Name who delivered him from the hands of his enemies
For on the day of his going before the Pope two mouths spoke to him
and as he entered the outer gate of the city a messenger came out towards
him and told him the news   that the one who sought his life had died
sudden death   instant   in that very night he was slain   and died
      and he was delivered   and then caught in Rome by the Little
Brothers   and stayed in their college "Strength" days [= 28]   and
went out on the first day of Marḥeshvan   and I have written this here to
say the praise of the Holy One Blessed Is He and His miracles and wonders
with Raziel and His faithful servants   H.L.

Accused of charlatanism & messianic claims, Abulafia fled to the desolate island of Comino (near Malta), developed a system of lettristic meditation ("Path of the Names") toward prophecy & communion with God. (See above, page 219.)

(Hebrew, medieval)

THE RAINBOW CALENDAR OF ISAAC LURIA

. . . & I have set my rainbow in the cloud
(Genesis 9.13.)

N I S A N   if you see the rainbow from the east side · an eastern king grows angry with his minister · & if the west · beasts in the field to die · wool be abundant & grapes & lentils bring success :

I Y A R   if from the east side · the world stays on its course three years · & if the west side · a western king to turn against his minister · & he will seize his wealth · beasts in the wilderness to die · much rainfall :

S I V A N   if from the east side · heavy sadness for the nations & much rain · & a famine in the land of Persia · & if in the west much wheat throughout the world :

T A M U Z   if from the east side · nations will be destroyed · thereafter peace & quiet in the land · & if the west side · forecast of good things for the poor & destitute :

A V   if from the east side · famine throughout the world & emptiness of pocket & war between the kings of Egypt & Media at the end they will make peace · & if the west side · famine in Media lasts three years · speakers of lies to multiply :

E L U L   if from the east side · war in Persia with the men of India & the men of India succeeding · & if the west side · successes in the villages :

T I S H R E I   if from the east side • great bounty in Assyria & in Rome • & death will be throughout the world • & if the west • great quarrels break out in the world • slaves to rebel against their masters :

H E S H V A N   if from the east side • & stars are visible by day this sign shows famine there will be death three years • & if the west side • a certain king to kill another :

K I S L E V   if from the east side • wheat in abundance & all sorts of seeds • & it will rain three months • & this foretells a sickness among men • & if the west • a certain king to go to war & to succeed :

T E V E T   if from the east side • a king will catch hold of overcome & kill the men who caught him • & the vineyards will succeed • & if the west • fruits will succeed & in Media wars :

S H E V A T   if from the east side • great abundance comes • & a king his princes & his soldiers go to war against a western king • & if the west • fruits will succeed • & in Media many wars :

A D A R   if from the east side • much rain in the desert • & travelers will succeed • & if the west • the rain to multiply to fullness • great sorrow in the deserts

J . R . / H . L .

COMMENTARY

While the calendar is obviously pseudepigraphic, it relates to the sense of catastrophe, etc. in Luria's great myth of exile (the "breaking of the vessels," for which see page 58, above). "From a historical point of view, Luria's myth constitutes a response to the expulsion of the Jews from Spain, an event which more than any other in Jewish history down to the catastrophe of our time gave urgency to the question: why the exile of the Jews and what is their vocation in the world? This question, the question of the meaning of the Jews' experience in exile, . . . lies indeed at the heart of the new conceptions which are the essence of Luria's system." (G. Scholem, *On the Kabbalah & Its Symbolism*, page 110.)

(Yiddish, 17th century)

"1648": FOR COSSACKS

                  bitter times
the cossack Krivno
        in the town of Bar
stood with Lysenko
all those decent people
       set a cross up
       led our brothers
       doomed men   broken boned
       out of a dark pit
       a black grave
Krivno who comforts them
says
       "spoke to your old men
       "your bosses
says it   gives forth a laugh
       "now I speak final words
       "both for my men & you
       "whose wives & children
       "suffer long from
       "hunger   thirst   cold
       "ask you to bow to
       "cross   end blindnesses
       "happily live on earth
Jews answer
       "silence   evil man
       "no other words
       "better you kill us here
       "no change of minds   nay nay
       "mind's bright as sunlight
       "evil man   can't work it
       "mind knows no other faith
       "though we be cut up   burnt
       "at stake et cetera
image of terror

follows
o genocide for Holy Name
& leaves a desert
wilderness
strewn with the bones of
Jewish prey

J.R.

COMMENTARY

The source of the song was the peasant & Cossack uprising led by Bogdan Chmielnicki against Polish rule in the Ukraine. Allied with the Polish nobility, the Jews suffered greatly in the attendant massacres – a trauma which influenced the messianism of Sabbatai Zevi & Jacob Frank, the emergence of Hasidism, etc.

Nathan of Gaza (Hebrew, c. 1643–80)

From THE VISION OF RABBI ABRAHAM:
THE BIRTH & CIRCUMSTANCES
OF THE MESSIAH SABBATAI ZEVI

& I Abraham had shut myself in for 40 years had grieved over the power of the Great Dragon lying in the middle of his rivers when *the voice of my beloved knocketh* saying look a son is born to Mordecai Zevi in the year 5386 & they will call him Sabbatai Zevi he will conquer the Great Dragon take the strength out of the piercing serpent & the crooked serpent he will be the true messiah : while I still was wondering at this vision look a man appeared to me he looked like polished brass from his loins on down he had the brightness of a fire from his loins on up was like bdellium transparent like the body of the sky he called LOOSEN THE KNOTS OF THE DEMONIC POWERS MAKE WAR AGAINST THEM & PRE-PARE A REFUGE THERE ARE NO PROVISIONS HERE : I fell into a deep sleep then a horror of great darkness over Egypt then a ferret & chameleon appeared & brought a great light *light that hides his power* & a man was there his size was one square cubit & his beard one cubit long his penis was a cubit & a span he held a hammer in his hand & tore up a great mountain ten by six score thousands & the man went up the mountain where a pit was that went down it to the bottom & he fell & fell inside : the man who looked like polished brass said don't you grieve over Messiah's fall for you will see the power of this man only now I couldn't hold my grief in now I fell into a heavy sleep I saw no other vision for a month

*

... blessed are thou o lord our god king of the
universe who permittest that which is forbidden.

(s . z .)

COMMENTARY

Nathan of Gaza – here working under the pseudonym of a 13th-century sage named Rabbi Abraham – was the prophet ("holy lamp") of the 17th-century messiah Sabbatai Zevi. The sabbatean movement itself survived Sabbatai's "fall" & conversion to Islam, reinterpreting it as a step toward that liberation from the "cruel commands," etc. to which it was germinal & which it helped bring about in later centuries. The Serpent, here & in the songs that follow, is a symbol both of the Messiah's enemy & of Sabbatai himself as Liberator. A development of Luria's kabbala, its relation to "the central symbol of the first- and second-century gnostic sect known as Ophites, or Naasenes" is also inescapable.

(Ladino, after 17th century)

3 POEMS FOR SABBATAI ZEVI [SHABTAI TSVI]
THE TRUE MESSIAH AS DRAWN FROM HYMNS
SUNG BY HIS FAITHFUL FOLLOWERS AFTER HIS
CONVERSION TO ISLAM FOR THE GREATER
GLORY OF THE GOD OF ISRAEL:

... I am the Lord your God Shabtai Tsvi

1

a glow of true messiah
whose faithful saw joy   light
his rising from the nether depths
spear set on rock
o he was light
was hidden   drowning in the sea
struck the crooked serpent
swallowed oil – was pure
oil of messiah –
day that they stole his clothing
from the sea of blood
then dressed up with his crown
cast lots for it
they called it "purim"
Barzilay his strong disciple crying
crying until night
who brought him clothing from his house
– for gayness to King David's son –

2

was born   the child of life
lit up high mountains
days since he crushed that snake
lit up high mountains
lit up the moon by daylight
redeemer who wore his crown

lit up high mountains
darkness was here no longer
– had not come from holy places –
redeemer showed the way the torah
lit up high mountains
was born   the sun that heals
healed the Shekinah
her wisdom came on us
lit up high mountains
he MY REMEMBRANCE says   I'm faithful
to believers in Zevi Sultan
my belief in him a tree
lit up high mountains
days since he crushed that snake
lit up high mountains
lit up the moon by daylight

3

. . . .

Sabbatai is myrrh root
is King David Jesse's son
the fourth leg of the chariot
went down into the sea
fought Samael
the king said   living   being

. . . .

opened the jet for us
freed us from cruel commands
expunged all griefs
King Sabbatai Zevi

J.R. / H.L.

COMMENTARY

Songs largely of the Dönmeh sect, i.e. of the Sephardic "believers" who followed
Sabbatai Zevi into Islam & a life as covert Jews. The Shekinah (Matronita) – as
God's (mythically female) presence on earth – was given concrete form in the
person of Sabbatai's third wife, Sarah ("prostitute" & "convert," in fulfillment of

Hosea: "Take a wife of whoredoms"), but later identified with Sabbatai himself. (Compare Eve, the daughter of Jacob Frank, below, & Helen, the companion of Simon Magus, 2nd-century gnostic messiah.) For the account of Sabbatai's battle with the serpent, loss & recovery of clothes, etc. (an event celebrated as a new Purim), see Scholem, *Sabbatai Ṣevi,* pages 145 – 46.

(Yiddish, traditional)

THE SONG OF THE SEXTON

---

                                    at dawn going from house to house &
                                       knocking at the shutters chanting:

get up jews
sweet holy jews
get up bow down to god
god is in exile
shekinah is in exile
the people is in exile
get up work for god

Jacob Frank (Hebrew / Polish, 1726–91)

From THE BOOK OF THE SAYINGS OF THE LORD

[These are some of the sayings of Yankiev Leivitch, Yakov ben Lev, who called himself Yakov Frank and whom some called Wise Jacob. Frank was a creature of Podolia, Turkey, Poland-in-its-disintegration. He traveled. His father was a traveling preacher. Frank was a peddler too and spoke everybody's language: Balkan, Turkish, Yiddish, Polish, Ladino, with quotations, citations, and language play from Hebrew and Aramaic. He joined up with Sabbateans, followers of the messianic movement begun by Shabtai Zvi and Nathan of Gaza, continued through Barukhya, and temporarily short one messiah. With them, he turned against the Talmud, into the Zohar, and out through the Sabbatean pore. He added some things to the movement: a new emphasis on the Virgin, a passage through Christianity, after the passage through Islam which Shabtai/ Nathan originated, on the way to Esau. Perhaps more sex. He became a messiah to thousands of Jews. – H.L.]

It is in your ancient books   that there is an island hidden in the sea
        & that by it a very great ship waits   full of weapons   & on that
island live kabbalistic Jews   awe-filled & devoted   & every month
they take boats out to the great ship to ask & seek if the time has come for
them to go out to the four corners of the world to wage war   On that
same island there is a great & very fearful mountain   that no man can
ascend   & on the mountain there is a golden staff   A strange man
will come & strike the ship   & then the hour will have come to begin the
war

I must wipe out your names   Even your sons will not be called by your
names   I give you new names   you & your sons

There is no other people in the whole world has gone as bad as the Jews
... They're like snakes & vipers   no love   no friendship   no
peace among them   only hate and strife   I have brought you out
from the midst of the Jews so that you might not learn to do as they do

My uncle Yakov told me that when I was a 2-year-old & he would take
me to his bed I would keep him up till he said "Good night" with me to all
the creatures: to big spiders & little ones   to all the snakes   to the
animals in the woods   to the birds   I said "Good night" to all of them

When I was little I saw a children's book   All the customs were
written in it   & there were different pictures   like pharaoh washing
in children's blood & so forth   We children took a knife & began
piercing & gashing not only what was bad but everything that was good as
well   until we made that book a sieve

In Sniatyn I saw that the beadle was accustomed to go from house to
house & would rap three times with the hammer in his hand to announce
penitence   So I gave him a few coins & he gave me the hammer   I
got up at midnight & went from house to house   from Jews to peasants
      from peasants to palaces   even to a well-known nobleman & to
Catholic priests & to all the inhabitants of the city & woke them from their
sleep   They were alarmed & all of them got up & called out in a loud
voice "What do you want?"   & I answered them "Arise for penitence!"
      & they ran after me & I fled   & I rapped twice on a Jewish gate &
they woke up & called "Blessed is the True Judge" & asked me "Who
died?"

When I saw the sight it seemed to me I heard a voice call "Go & lead
Jacob the Wise to the Chambers   & when you bring him to the First
Chamber I warn you   the command is upon you   to open all the
windows & doors before him   So there I was flying in the wind & on my
right & left were two virgins the like of whose beauty has never been seen
      In those chambers I saw mostly women & Virgins   in a few of them
there were groups of teachers & students   & when I had heard just one
word of their discourse I immediately understood everything they intended
to say   & there were many of these Chambers & in the last I saw the
First (I mean Shabtai Zvi) seated as well   like a teacher with his stu-
dents   wearing the clothes of a Frank   & he turned to me & asked
"Are you this Jacob the Wise? I have heard about you   that you're a
hero & have soul   I too went to the place you're going   but I don't
have the strength to go on   If you want to   be strong!   & the
Name will help you   Many Fathers have taken this burden on & failed
      & there he showed me through the window a depth like the Black Sea
covered in a fearsome dark   & to the side of the depth I saw a great
mountain   reaching up into the heart of the sky   & I called out

"Come what may!
I'm going!
God help me!"

Another time   I came to the synagogue in Salonika where around
1200 well-to-do Jews were gathered   & the gabbai called men up to the

Torah   "Let such-&-such get up" according to the custom of the place
        & I called out in a loud voice "Don't a single one of you dare come up
to the Torah   or I'll kill him & lay him waste right here!
    When they heard this awful impudence all of them became disturbed &
began to grumble & mutter against me
    So then I grabbed the lectern in front of me & warned them again that I
would murder any man who moved up to the Torah with the lectern & then
I took the scroll of the Torah & sat on it . . .
    & the Jews were completely terrified & fled from the synagogue

Today you make fun of me   but I tell you that the number of Jews
that will follow me will be as great as the hairs on your heads

Since I could find no lodging I was forced to curl up in sewers & caves &
to spend the night lying in refuse   I bore all this & suffered it on account
of my love for the Name   to do His will

    . . . but the sea would not take me & vomited me up on to the dry land

I will go & I will enter Poland   for the place of the Ascent is in Poland
        There a building will be built   more beautiful than man has seen
since the world was created

There is a certain tree whose branches are spread out behind the wall
which surrounds it   & whoever looks at the wall from the outside seems
to see many trees   But he who sees from behind the fence knows that
there is no more than one tree there   So we must know & desire one
tree & not seek many trees

When the water is turbid it is good to catch fish   & so when the world
is filled with bloodshed we will be able to hunt the thing that belongs to us

    . . . the Shekhina . . . the Virgin . . . most beautiful of women

You see my daughter   Know that she is a queen!   But do not
think that it is on account of her beauty we call her "queen"
    No!   She is really a queen   In reality

This world is the Gate of Shells   Every grain has a shell that encloses
it   You see that the whole world calls out "Eternal Virgin!"   says
that she is the Redeemer & Savior   She has suffered alongside Him
since the beginning & has had no place of rest   & has gone wandering

with Him & has fled with Him to Egypt   She comes before the fruit which will come into the world soon   that all the kings of the world will bow to

when you hear that I'm in great distress & that the people walking behind me are in trouble & being chased from place to place & are without bread or clothes   know that it's God leading us

Eve tells me that there's a treasure in the mountain   six hundred million pieces of gold the Catholic priests know nothing of   & I wanted to order you to go to a certain cave near Czestochowa   & there you'd have found six hundred tailors sewing clothes   & on every garment gold coins would be attached so loosely that when one wearing them passed through the streets gold coins would fall off   & the people would come running from right & left to gather the coins   & I would have ordered that the clothes be made ready & the carriages before we left the prison
     but we would have taken nothing from the treasure & only would have divided it out among the believers according to their needs   & when we left the prison I would have been sitting with her in the carriage & no man would've seen her but me & you   & as we passed through the streets of Warsaw the gold would've fallen left & right   & all the people of Warsaw would've been gathering up the gold   & you would've called out in a mighty voice "Long live the King!"   & all the lords & people would've called "Here is our King!"

One day he asked those who know the secrets   Issakhar & Morde-khai   to explain Shabtai Zvi's death   The men said to him

> Shabtai Zvi came to taste everything in the world
> So of course
> he had to taste the bitterness of death

But he said

> The answer is good
> But if he came to taste it all
> why did he not taste the sweetness
> of rule & reign

I will teach you the manners of kingship   for I want to give a crown to every one of you

In a dream in Czestochowa I saw the goddess who came to me appearing as a beautiful virgin   & I brought you before Her   & when you came you turned back at the door & two of you fell to the earth   & when they came back again She leaned Her head away from one of them completely & from the other only partially   & for this reason I have not rejected him completely   Be unified from now on & heed me   perhaps the salvation will come again   I have brought you to the nations   it's a custom of theirs to plow in order to seed   & now that you've spread scandal & revealed this secret to the nations you have driven me out of the inheritance of the Name in Poland

I tell you that all the Jews are in big trouble now because they wait for the coming of the Redeemer & not the coming of the Maiden   Look upon the peoples how they dwell peaceably in their possessions for they trust their Maiden   who is only the reflection of the image of our Maiden

When people change their faith what's it like? Like pouring oil from cruse to cruse   Thus I left the faith of Ishmael & entered the Christian faith & hid it from no man that I was previously of Ishmaelite faith The day will yet come when I return to it again   & then my holy name will be revealed to all the world

When the Name comes to my aid I will buy a beautiful house & fill it with beautiful furnishings & set special rooms apart for my daughter & dress her in queenly robes & precious jewels   & I will not permit any man to come near her   only I myself will take pleasure in her & I'll drink & eat with her   & only when gentile guests come will I invite them to eat with her too   & I'll sit with her day & night & tell her what I know so she will come to understand the greatness of our faith   For until today I have not said even one thing about it to her   It's in my mind to raise her up to the status of a man / an adam so everything that's happened to me will happen to her

In a dream I saw the Christian lawmaker sitting   & around him Catholic priests   by a fountain of good pure water   & when I looked closely I saw that the fountain flowed out from there & came to me

I say to you   that even if all the kings of all the nations come to me it is nothing in my eyes   My sole intent & desire is that the Jews come to me   The Jews are destined to come to me in multitudes   No rank of the camp will be less than ten thousand   Every troop will have its own flag in its own colors   the black flag & the blue will come last   On the flags new things will be revealed & seen   & the world is destined to come to me & say what they saw on the flags

You are invited to come under my flag   because we will be
marching towards a known thing with this flag   & therefore I have
called you my brothers   because you're destined to be my flag bearers
    & I too will carry the flag   though my hands are heavy   I say to
you : when these Jews come   you must go out to meet them humbly &
meekly   your heads & eyes to the ground   & then you will come to
know what the Name has done in His world

H.L.

(Yiddish, traditional)

FIVE FOR THE REBBE

1

The rebbe went dancing
& lost all he had
When his hasidim found it
he gave them a sign
Then he took it all back

2

The rebbe was a good old boy
when he drank a toast
all his hasidim used to fight
to catch the droppings

3

When the rebbe dances
the walls dance with him
the hasidim clap hands
They clap hands when the rebbe dances

4

The rebbe sits & sweats
& the shekinah hovers over him

Then the hasidim sing & dance & jump
They love the way the rebbe looks

5

days of messiah
king   the rebbe
eldest
wears his hair long
like a hermit
sweet bread   buns
grow on the trees
with corn cob pipes
for branches
& tobacco leaves
hasidim can light up on
not in prayer huts
made of clay brick
but built with
stews & noodle puddings
whiskey fountains
in the rebbe's kitchen
Nebukhadnezzar
come himself from Babylon
into Yerushelayim
crying to the rebbe
life   life
all that they drink is life

                                                        J . R .

COMMENTARY

(1) Songs by proponents & enemies of hasidism, an ecstatic branch of orthodox
Judaism, founded in the 18th century by Israel ben Eliezer, the Baal Shem Tov (or
"Master of the Good Name"). The movement, which formed communities around
charismatic *rebbes* or *tsadikim* (= "saints"), is commonly viewed as a response
within Judaism to the Sabbateans, etc. In the songs given here the line between
reverence & scorn is already very thin.

(2) "'All rabbis look like savages,' Langer said." (F. Kafka.)

Rajzel Zychlinska (Yiddish, b. 1910)

POOR PEOPLE

Being poor has one color
Everywhere.
Poor people walk over the earth silently
Speaking to the worms.
From beneath all the rocks
Death looks at them
And calls.

LUCY S. DAWIDOWICZ & FLORENCE VICTOR

(Anonymous, Yiddish)

ZARITSKY'S CHILDREN, & OTHER POEMS
FOR THE RICH

1

Zaritsky with 10 children
10 children
the rest of us who sweat
to feed them
woe o woe o wind
sweet children
locked in his factories
o worse off than his dog

2

derision of the working class
the poor
what was a working girl to them

o money   money's
wisdom in this world
past all reproach

3

o mother o mother
cat's licking the butter
hen's laying eggs
bride's got a veil
groom wears a prayer-shawl
poor man stays poor
children suck fingers
women die starving

4

bosses with hearts of stone
lived in distrust of
workers   a poor working man
would drink a little whiskey
called him a drunkard
to his face
              cheap whiskey was
their wine   a golden goblet
is no cup
a working man's no master
in his house
o fatherer of worlds
where does it end?

5

A POEM FOR MILLIONAIRES

viz Rothschild   face of gold
conspicuous consumer
died like any beggar
once went to his vault
for money   speculation
trapped inside
all doors were closing on him
seven days of hunger   sucked

blood from his own fingers
Rothschild   Rothschild
strutted before kings
he said he couldn't die
of hunger
ended like the rest
he lies there
broken into pieces
bag of bones

J.R.

*

*Samuel said, & some say, Rav Joseph: Poverty is becoming to Jews, like a red
halter on a white horse.*

Peretz Markish (Yiddish, 1895–1952)

Two Poems

I

I don't know whether I'm at home
or homeless.
              I'm running, my shirt
unbuttons, no bounds, nobody
holds me, no beginning,
no end

my body is foam
smelling of wind

                         Now
is my name. I spread my arms, my hands
pierce the extremes
of what is. I'm letting my eyes roam around

and do their drinking from the foundations
of the world

eyes wild, shirt ballooning,
my hands separated by the world, I don't know
if I have a home
or have a homelessness,
or am a beginning or an end

2

I won't put on a light all night
the wall disappears in tears and quiet
from the blue dovecot of my prayed-out face

ripped out of my eyes, the dove,
by itself, and gone.
                    A rope
circles my head. My head is the shame
under a rope. And my hands, my cheated hands . . .

loneliness, I'll make up a bed for us
on the threshold. Would you
caress me? if you would caress me, caress
me

will the dove come back in the morning?
she will. I'll kiss you, world, your fingers,
and close my eyes
and splash out
your blue secret.
                    Thank you, God.

the wild dove ripped itself
from my eyes. It flew. Somewhere my walls
walked quietly off.
and where did you hide your hands?

I won't put on a light all night
in the blue dovecot of my mourned-out face.

ARMAND SCHWERNER

Jacob Glatstein (Yiddish, 1896–1971)

GOOD NIGHT, WORLD

Good night, wide world,
big stinking world.
Not you but I slam shut the gate.
With a long gaberdine,
with a fiery yellow patch,
with a proud stride,
because I want to,
I'm going back to the ghetto.
Wipe away, stamp out every vestige of conversion.
I roll around in your garbage—
praise, praise, praise—
hunchbacked Jewish life.
Damn your dirty culture, world.
I wallow in your dust
even though it's forsaken,
sad Jewish life.
German pig, cutthroat Pole,
Rumania, thief, land of drunkards and gluttons.
Weak-kneed democracy, with your cold
sympathy-compresses.
Good night, electrified arrogant world.
Back to my kerosene, candle shadows,
eternal October, tiny stars,
to my crooked streets, humped lanterns,
my sacred pages, my Bible,
my Gemorra, to my backbreaking
studies, to the bright Yiddish prayerbook,
to law, profundity, duty, justice—
world, I walk gladly towards quiet ghetto light.

Good night. I'll make you, world, a gift of
all my liberators.
Take back your Jesus-Marxes, choke on their courage.
Croak over a drop of our Christianized blood.
For I have hope, even if He is delaying,

day by day my expectation rises.
Green leaves will yet rustle
on our sapless tree.
I don't need any consolation.
I'm going back to my very beginnings,
from Wagner's pagan music to melody, to humming.
I kiss you, dishevelled Jewish life,
I cry with the joy of coming back.

August 1938

RUTH WHITMAN

*when night fell the stars glittered   the pile of corpses lay in the field   &
snow came down out of the night with soft cruel abundance • such was God's will
• the presence of a god was felt but it belonged to the goyim • there is a god in the
world but there is no god of Israel*   (Uri Zvi Greenberg)

Paul Celan (German, 1920–70)

A DEATH FUGUE

Black milk of morning we drink you at dusktime
we drink you at noontime & dawntime we drink you at night
we drink & drink
we scoop out a grave in the sky where it's roomy to lie
There's a man in this house who cultivates snakes & who writes
who writes when it's nightfall *nach Deutschland* your golden hair Margareta
he writes it & walks from the house & the stars all start flashing he whistles
       his dogs to draw near
whistles his Jews to appear starts us scooping a grave out of sand
he commands us play up for the dance

Black milk of morning we drink you at night
we drink you at dawntime & noontime we drink you at dusktime

we drink & drink
There's a man in this house who cultivates snakes & who writes
who writes when it's nightfall *nach Deutschland* your golden hair Margareta
your ashen hair Shulamite we scoop out a grave in the sky where it's roomy
    to lie

He calls jab it deep in the soil you men you other men sing & play
he tugs at the sword in his belt & swings it his eyes are blue
jab your spades deeper you men you other men play up again for the dance

Black milk of morning we drink you at night
we drink you at noontime & dawntime we drink you at dusktime
we drink & drink
there's a man in this house your golden hair Margareta
your ashen hair Shulamite he cultivates snakes
He calls play that death thing more sweetly Death is a gang-boss *aus*
    Deutschland
he calls scrape that fiddle more darkly then hover like smoke in the air
then scoop out a grave in the clouds where it's roomy to lie

Black milk of morning we drink you at night
we drink you at noontime Death is a gang-boss *aus Deutschland*
we drink you at dusktime & dawntime we drink & drink
Death is a gang-boss *aus Deutschland* his eye is blue
he hits you with leaden bullets his aim is true
there's a man in this house your golden hair Margareta
he sets his dogs on our trail he gives us a grave in the sky
he cultivates snakes & he dreams Death is a gang-boss *aus Deutschland*

your golden hair Margareta
your ashen hair Shulamite

J.R.

Uri Zvi Greenberg (Hebrew, b. 1894)

From GOD IN EUROPE

We were not like dogs among the Gentiles ... they pity a dog,
They pet him, even kiss him with the Gentile mouth.
Like a fat baby, one of their very own,
They pamper him, always laughing and playing;
And when the dog dies, how bitterly the Gentiles mourn him!

We were not brought in boxcars like lambs to the slaughter,
Rather, like leprous sheep,
Through all the beautiful landscapes of Europe,
They shipped us to Death.
They did not handle their sheep as they handled our bodies;
They did not yank out their teeth before they killed them;
Nor strip the wool from their bodies as they stripped our skin;
Nor shovel them into the fire to make ashes of their life,
And scatter the ashes over streams and sewers.

Where are there other analogies to this,
This monstrous thing we suffered at their hands?
There *are* none – no other analogies! (All words are shadows of shadows) –
That is the horror: no other analogies!
No matter how brutal the torture a man may endure in a Christian country,
He who comes to compare will compare it thus:
He was tortured like a Jew.
Every fear, every anguish, every loneliness, every agony,
Every scream, every weeping in this world,
He who compares things will say:
This is the Jewish kind.

There is no retribution for what they did to us –
Its circumference is the world:
The culture of Christian kingdoms to its peak
Is covered with our blood,
And all their conscience, with our tears.

ROBERT MEZEY

Yehuda Amichai (Hebrew, b. 1924)

NATIONAL THOUGHTS

You: trapped in the homeland of the Chosen People.
On your head a cossack's fur hat,
Child of their pogroms.
"After these words." Always.
Or, for instance, your face: slanting eyes,
Pogrom-Year eyes. Your cheekbones, high,
Hetman's cheekbones, Hetman the rabble-king.
Hassid dancing, dutiful, you, naked on a rock in the early evening by the
    canopies of water at Ein Geddi
With eyes closed and your body open like hair.
After these words, "Always."
Every day I know the miracle of
Jesus walking upon the waters,
I walk through my life without drowning.

To speak, now, in this tired language
Torn from its sleep in the Bible –
Blinded, it lurches from mouth to mouth –
The language which described God and the Miracles,
Says:
Motor car, bomb, God.
The squared letters wanted to stay closed,
Every letter a locked house,
To stay and to sleep in it forever.

                                    ASSIA GUTMANN

Allen Ginsberg (b. 1926)

JAWEH AND ALLAH BATTLE

Jaweh with Atom bomb
    Allah cuts throat of Infidels
Jaweh's armies beat down neighboring tribes
Will Red Sea waters close & drown th'armies of Allah?

Israel's tribes worshipping the Golden Calf
    Moses broke the Tablets of Law.

Zalmon Schacter Lubovitcher Rebbe what you say
    Stone Commandments broken on the ground
  Sufi Sam whaddya say
    Shall Prophet's companions dance circled
      round Synagogue while Jews doven bearded electric?

Both Gods Terrible! Awful Jaweh Allah!
    Both hook-nosed gods, circumcized.
Jaweh Allah which unreal?
        Which stronger Illusion?
         Which stronger Army?
     Which gives most frightening command?
What God maintain egohood in Eden? Which be Nameless?
      Which enter Abyss of Light?
Worlds of Gods, jealous Warriors, Humans, Animals & Flowers,
    Hungry Ghosts, even Hell Beings all die,
   Snake cock and pig eat eachother's tails & perish
All Jews all Moslems'll die all Israelis all Arabs
Cairo's angry millions Jerusalem's multitudes
    suffer Death's dream Armies in battle!
Yea let Tribes wander to tin camps at cold Europe's walls?
Yea let the Million sit in desert shantytowns with tin cups?
I'm a Jew cries Allah! Empty Buddha circumcized!
      Snake sneaking apple to Eden—
   Alien, Wanderer, Caller of the Great Call!
What Prophet born on this ground
      bound me Eternal to Palestine

circled by Armies tanks, droning bomber motors,
radar electric computers?
What Mind directed Stern Gang Irgun Al Fatah Black September?
Meyer Lansky? Nixon Shah? Gangster? Premier? King?
one-eyed General Dayan?
Golda Meir & Kissinger bound me with Arms?
HITLER AND STALIN SENT ME HERE!
WEITZMANN & BEN-GURION SENT ME HERE!
NASSER AND SADAT SENT ME HERE!
ARAFAT SENT ME HERE! MESSIAH SENT ME HERE!
GOD SENT ME HERE!
Buchenwald sent me here! Vietnam sent me here!
My-Lai sent me here!
Lidice sent me here!
My mother sent me here!
I WAS BORN HERE IN ISRAEL, Arab
circumcized, my father had a coffee shop in Jerusalem
One day the Soldiers came & told me to walk down road
my hands up
walk away leave my house business forever!
The Israelis sent me here!
Solomon's Temple the Pyramids & Sphinx sent me here!
JAWEH AND ALLAH SENT ME HERE!
Abraham will take me to his bosom!
Mohammed will guide me to Paradise!
Christ sent me here to be crucified!
Buddha will wipe us out and destroy the world.
The New York Times and Cairo Editorialist Heykal sent me here!
Commentary and *Palestine Review* sent me here!
The International Zionist Conspiracy sent me here!
Syrian Politicians sent me here! Heroic Pan-Arab
Nationalists sent me here!
They're sending Armies to my side —
The Americans & Russians are sending bombing planes tanks
Chinese Egyptians Syrians help me battle for my righteous
house my Soul's dirt Spirit's Nation body's
boundaries & Self's territory my
Zionist homeland my Palestine inheritance
The Capitalist Communist & Third World Peoples
Republics Dictatorships Police States Socialisms & Democracies
are all sending Deadly Weapons to our aid!
We shall triumph over the Enemy!

Maintain our Separate Identity! Proud
History evermore!
Defend our own bodies here this Holy Land! This hill
Golgotha never forget, never relinquish
inhabit thru Eternity
under Allah Christ Yaweh forever one God
Shema Yisroel Adonoi Eluhenu Adonoi Echad!
La ilah illa' Allah hu!
OY!   AH! HU!   OY!   AH!   HU!
SHALOM!   SHANTIH!   SALAAM!

January 13, 1974

Jerome Rothenberg (b. 1931)
TERROR

. . . .

dream of the jews
has ended   something else
waits in its place
a gunman maybe
standing at your door
who watches
in back of his blood
the horse's eye
run through his mind
"a wolf" the killer
calls himself
offers his body, shyly
to the fathers
wakes at dawn, his eye
bigger than the moon
shines for him
& leads him down the hall
— hellos, exchange of dishes

fantasies of home –
the mouth of the fanatic
trembles   stutters
he is in love with his first dream
the taste of honey
cloth against his fingertips
traditions of their people
motors secret hideouts
his mother even now
whispers to his dark side
the letters of the universe
exploding lights
signal him on
he will address the bride
again   a lesson of his courage
he will give her
satisfaction
night & day
he circles around her
like a watchdog
prowling prowling
beside her father's stall
the gunman
speaks to his own shadow
on the hill
– depletion –
– death –
over the hill a camel
walks, stupidly
into the camera
stop him!
even if for a moment
cries the gunman's mouth
the teeth of the fanatic
biting staining the pale roots
the mask of antiochus
finds a jewish face
looks back at us
in righteousness
in anger at his own flesh
what can we give
but whispers

to make the rain appear?
the rain won't,
will it?
the daughter returns to the hut,
party ended,
bodies propped on bare beds
the fanatic's kin
his victims
tunnels exploded through their hearts
fly past him
foam pours from his mouth
his lungs fill up with foam
the wounded deer flies past
& calls him
like his vanished thumbs
another landscape
opens
with his boot he presses
legs & back
moving the flesh aside
& probes – aloof – the thin line
where the legs meet
grown thick with hair
how tight the dreamer's hand
becomes   how close
to prayer
his angry copulations
the mind of the fanatic
fills with glass   the fish
swim in the broken auto
furniture & rags
ignited
clot the hallways
processions of pale jews
are arabs now
the gunman, dark fanatic
gentile become jew
jew gentile
bellows in broken hebrew
in accents of his childhood
southern towns
assassins & vigilantes

even his mother can't believe
the coming struggle
treasons against god
repelled
forever   the killer
born to kill
escapes from the viet nam tunnel
in the street of little jewelers
semites of his mind
he rides a hairy motor bike
(the friend says)
gun slung over chest
into a world of strangers
caftaned killers
heavy with arab names
who wait for him
will stage the final shootout
the clock is moving
toward its end
explosions at the father's grave
the decade is a thrill for them
a new encounter
bigger than the last
the blood is such a clock
& such a clock
is always throbbing
in the blood
& in the morning sky

COMMENTARY

On May 2, 1980, Palestinian gunmen ambushed a group of Israeli settlers on the
occupied West Bank. Among the six Israelis killed was Eli Hazeez (the last name
means "the wolf"), born James Eli Mahon, Jr., in Alexandria, Virginia. An Amer-
ican Protestant by birth, he came out of Viet Nam & American ultraconservatism
into Israeli citizenship & conversion through the right-wing Kach movement led by
Meir Kahane. During his stay in Israel, the *N.Y. Times* reported, "he was jailed for 8
months for breaking into Arab houses in Hebron, smashing furniture, beating resi-
dents, and shouting at them to get out of 'Jewish houses.'" Of those who died in the
ambush, "he alone was buried defiantly in the Jewish Cemetery of occupied Arab
Hebron."

Semite: to find a way for myself.
(G. Oppen)

George Oppen (1908–1984)
SEMITE

---

what art and anti-art to lead us by the sharpness

of its definitions connected
to all other things this is the bond

sung to all distances

my distances neither Roman

nor barbarian the sky the low sky

of poems precise
as the low sky

that women have sung from the windows
of cities sun's light

on the sills a poetry

of the narrow
end of the funnel proximity's salt gales in the narrow

end of the funnel the proofs

are the images the images
overwhelming earth

rises up

in its light nostalgia
of the mud guilts

of the foxhole what is a word a name at the
   limits

of devotion
to life the terrible knowledge

of deception

a lie told my loves tragically
pitifully had deceived

themselves had been betrayed

demeaned thrown away shamed
degraded

stripped naked Think

think also of the children
the guards laughing

the one pride the pride
of the warrior laughing so the hangman
comes to all dinners Aim

we tell each other the children cannot be
    alone whereupon murder

comes to our dinners poem born

of a planet the size

of a table top
garden   forest   an awning

fluttering four-lane

highway the instant

in the open the moving
edge and one
is I

THE END OF "A BOOK OF THE WARS OF YAHVEH"

THE WRITINGS

ג

Tradition, according to its mystical sense, is Oral Torah, precisely because every stabilization in the text would hinder and destroy the infinitely moving, the constantly progressing and unfolding element within it, which would otherwise become petrified. The writing down and codification of the Oral Torah, undertaken in order to save it from being forgotten, was therefore not only a protective as (in the deeper sense) a pernicious act.

— GERSHOM SCHOLEM

The book is as old as water and fire.

— EDMOND JABÈS

A Book of Writings

I

(Hebrew, 10th century B.C.)

THE GEZER CALENDAR

---

the moons of harvest
the moons of sowing
the moons of late planting
the moon of reaping flax
the moon of reaping barley
the moon of reaping & measuring
the moons of vine-tending
the moon of summer (-fruit)

a

b

g

COMMENTARY

One of the earliest surviving Hebrew inscriptions, the "calendar" was engraved on a limestone tablet in ancient Hebrew script. Among other possibilities the content is described as "a popular folk song, listing the months of the year according to the agricultural seasons." (*Encyclopedia Judaica.*) Such functional lunar namings are widespread among American Indians, others.

(Canaanite / Hebrew, before 13th century B.C.)

YHVH'S BATTLE WITH THE SERPENT

1

Waken
Waken
Gird might of arm
YHVH
Waken as before endless generatings

Didn't you crush Rahab?
        hole Tannin?
Didn't you dry up Yam?
        mighty waters of Tehom?
        set the ⌠YAM deeps a path for the saved to tread?
            ⌊sea

2

In his might he stirred the ⌠sea
                    ⌊YAM
Then in his cunning crushed Rahab
By his wind set ⌠YAM in net
            ⌊sea
His hand made holes in the twisty snake

3

You broke up ⌠YAM in your might
           ⌊sea
You smashed Tanin-heads in the water
You crushed Leviatan heads
Made him food for desert folk
You split spring and creek
You dried up   mighty rivers
The ⌠day is yours
    ⌊yom

The night is yours
You set up light and sun
You determined earthbounds
Summer and winter
              you made them

H.L.

COMMENTARY

"These Canaanite-Hebrew texts are remnants of a Canaanite myth contained within the Hebrew Bible." With which, compare "The Battle between Yam & Baal" (Lenowitz and Doria, *Origins,* pages 273–75).

(Hebrew, Bible, 12th / 11th century B.C.)

THE SONG OF DEBORAH

Deborah sang that day
with Barak son of Avino'am
"of warriors who let their hair grow long
"in Israel
"when armies went to war
              (bless Yahveh)
"would have kings hear it
"would have chiefs listen
"I who sing to Yahveh
"I to Yahveh
"who play the string for Yahveh
"elohim of Israel
"you Yahveh when you went from Se'ir
"when you marched from Edom's fields
"earth shook
"the sky rained loudly
"loudly the clouds rained water

"hills flowed in front of Yahveh
                    you This-One-of-Sinai
            Yahveh elohim of Israel :
"in the days of Shamgar son of Anat
"days of Ya'el
                        roads were blocked
"travelers would go by winding roads
"arts of war were blocked in Israel
"blocked until you rose
"you Deborah you mother you in Israel
"when they took new gods
"war's meat hanging from the gates
            who saw a shield then
            or a spear?
"you 40 thousands in all Israel
"my heart is with the chiefs of Israel
"warriors in Israel
                    (bless Yahveh) :
"those who rode there on fine asses
"who sat on silks
"even those who walked the highways
            hear me
            hear the cymbals' voices
"between water troughs
"where Yahveh's holy deeds dropped down
"deeds of the warriors in Israel
"who went up to the gates with Yahveh :
            o stand up stand up
            Deborah
            stand up stand up o sing your song
"Barak step out & take your prisoners :
"when a handful went against great powers
"Yahveh's armies went with me
"against the warriors
                    some summoned from Efrayim
            roots in Amalek
"will be behind you Binyamin
"with all your troops
"from Makhir chieftains coming down
"others from Zevulun
"carried the warrior's club
"& princes of Issakhar were with Deborah

"were Barak's allies
"sent into the valley at his call :
"& Re'uven your divisions
"mighty heroes in their heads
"why did they sit it out between the sheepfolds
"why did they listen to the shepherds' flutes
"o Re'uven your divisions
"mighty talkers in their heads :
"while Gil'ad stayed put across the Jordan
"& Dan stuck to his ships
"& Asher kept beside the sea shore
"tight in his harbors
"only Zevulun mad to spill his life
"there with Naftali on the rises :
"kings came warring
"warring kings of Canaan
"in Ta'anakh by Megido's waters
"came but carried off no silver
"from the sky the stars fought
"fought with Sisra from their courses
"Kishon Brook has dragged them down
"a brook has mastered them
"you Kishon Brook that crushed strong spirits :
                    then a hammering
"of horses' hoofs in flight
"in galloping
"who galloped faster than his warriors :
"curse Meroz (Yahveh's angel says)
"curse those who live there
"who would not come to Yahveh's aid
"Yahveh's aid against the powers :
"but bless above all women
"Ya'el the wife of Kenite Heber
"more than the women in their tents
"her blessing   (sing)

     when he asked for water
     she gave him milk
     she brought it in a deep cup
     brought him curds
     her hand was on the spike
     her right hand on the heavy hammer

she brought it down on Sisra
she smashed his head
she crushed it
struck the spike into his neck
he bent down at her feet he fell
he fell he lay down at her feet
he bent down at her feet he fell
fell where he bent
he bent down at her feet he fell
he lay there ruined

(coda)

through her window Sisra's mother
looks & cries
& through her grill she asks
"why is his chariot
"so late coming
"why is the noise of chariots
"so late
her wisest princess tells her
is even echoing her words
"they must be
"splitting up the spoils
"one or two virgins
"for each man
"a spoil of colored cloth
"for Sisra
"embroidered colors for his spoil
"many clothes around my neck
"for spoil
O Yahveh Yahveh may your enemies
be lost
your lovers like the rising of the sun
in power

& so the land had rest
for forty years

J.R. / H.L.

A judge & prophetess in Israel circa 1200 – 1125 B.C., Deborah promoted a "war of liberation" against Jabin, king of Canaan. Her military commander, Barak, attacked the army of Sisra, a Canaanite general, & sank his chariots in the mire caused by Kishon's flooding. This led to Sisra's flight & murder at the hands of Ya'el, wife of an allied Kenite chieftain. From an actual oral tradition, the song was "probably sung antiphonally" or as a kind of (bardic) re-enactment. There is some possibility that the poet was a woman.

(Hebrew, Bible, c. 10th century B.C.)

From THE SONG OF SONGS

1

I came into my garden
saw my sister there
but saw her as my wife

I picked my sweet plant
ate my honeycomb with honey
drank my wine with milk

(I told them) eat, friends
drink & go on drinking
O sweet love

2

I slept
my heart was moving
heard her voice

a knocking at the door
(says) open for me
sister

love
my love
my dove
my head was wet
with dew   the night
bathed in my hair

3

he put his hand against
the keyhole

made me feel him
down my belly

4

I got up
I would let him in
my hands smelled sweet

my fingers
smelling sweet
against the lock

5

had opened for him
my sweet love
was gone   had left me

(says) he spoke
I felt my breath go
would look for him

but couldn't find him
& called to him
he didn't answer

6

is he more sweet
than others?
is she more beautiful?

is her sweet love
more beautiful?
has she told it to us right?

7

sometimes pale
he blushes
is better than 10,000 men

gold skin of forehead
bushy hair
& black   is like a crow

with dove's eyes
looking at a river
washed with milk
in perfect space

to hold his cheeks
a spice bed
his lips like lilies
breathing a sweet spice

through hands with gold rings
beryl at center
his belly is high ivory
& sapphire

marble legs
like columns into pure gold sockets
his face
a strength like cedar

sweetness at his mouth
"is altogether lovely
"is my sweet love
"is my friend

J.R.

The gathering is itself an anthology of erotic poem-songs, later allegorized but clearly related to the religio-sexual practices of the "alternative" Jewish cults, neighboring religions, etc. Compare, e.g., Sumerian & Egyptian love poetry recently recovered:

> When I leave you, my Brother, and feel your love,
>   my heart stalls within me.
> When I see sweet cakes, they turn to salt.
> Pomegranate-wine, once so delicious, is like bird's gall.
> The breath of your nostrils, nothing else frees my body.
> What I have found, may Amen grant me forever.

(Thus: Milton Kessler & Gerald E. Kadish, in "Love Songs & Tomb Songs of Ancient Egypt," *Alcheringa* 5, 1973.)

(Syriac / Greek, c. 200 A.D.)

THE MAIDEN

<pre>
                          I would sing of
who is daughter of light   on whom
brightness of kings does rest
I would delight in her image's rays
her beauty   whose garments
are flowers sweet odors rise from
a king looks out from her eyes
will feed those beneath him
in truth   truth covers her head
the tread of her feet brings pleasure
she spreads her lips open
for beauty   sings praise poems
32 singing her praises
tongue like a curtain the priest can raise up
& enter   her neck mounts high
like a staircase   first builder hung here
</pre>

her hands that were speaking
in code   led the dance of the aeons
fingers that opened the gates
to the city   whose chamber
vibrates with light
the odor of sweet leaves & myrrh
strewn with branches of myrtle   sweet flowers
a door decked with reeds
stand the seven who guarded the groom
whom she chose   seven bridesmaids
who dance for her praise her
twelve more by her count who are servants
attend her   their gaze
toward the bridegroom
sighting of whom brings them light
of the joy of their entry
those who would be at that marriage
assemblage of princes   long feasting
long lives of those given to life
wore garments of light splendid raiment
would swoon in their joy in praise of
father of all   take his light down
exult in it   light of their vision
of godlight
sweet food now received
sweet perfection sweet drink
of his wine   ends thirst   desire
bursts into praises o breath
o father of truths o mother of knowing

                                        J.R.

COMMENTARY

In other texts, "the maiden" is already allegorized into Church, etc.; here she retains the presence of Shekinah, Sophia, etc., or simply "maiden."

(Hebrew, 14th century)

A CHARM AGAINST LILITH

"Black Striga
            black on black
"who eats black blood
                    & drinks it
"like an ox she bellows
"like a bear she growls
"like a wolf she crushes

J.R.

COMMENTARY

"She told him she was Lilith & that if he let her go she would teach him all her names. The names she wrote down were

LILITH	ABITR	ABITO	AMORFO
KKODS	IKPODO	AYYLO	PTROTA
ABNUKTA	STRIGA	KALI	PTUZA
	TLTOI-PRITSA.		

He told her he was Elijah." (Traditional amulet). For more on Lilith as a "child-devouring female demon," etc., see pages 42 – 45, above.

(Yiddish, 20th century)

THE EVIL EYE (THE GOOD EYE) EINEHORE

The child frets
yawns
or cringes a lot

The adult
yawns
"he just doesn't feel good"

or
they have a cold or a flu
"a light disease"

II DIAGNOSIS

The mother or the grandmother goes and
licks out the eyes

"the child has einehore   the eyes are salty"

"She takes a glass of water
and charcoal

She puts in three pieces of charcoal

If they fall down
If they sink ... "

or
"You take a glass of water
You put three or four twigs on top of the glass
Crack an egg over the branches

If the egg sticks in them ... "

or
"Hold a new knife at the head
If it turns black ... "

     III T R E A T M E N T

By charm
       in silence
       in whispers
       facing east

Schneider:
       "I once asked
       'Tell me what it is woman
       what a good eye means

       How do you cast out a good eye?'

       She says
       'This is a secret'

       I say
       'Teach me the secret   I should know too'

       She says
       'I am only an old Jewish woman
       Should I teach you to cast out a good eye?
       It's nothing with nothing
       One time it may succeed
       and one time it may not succeed'

       She teaches me
       She says:
            'Woe is the child
            'So is the mama'

       She takes the corner of her dress or apron
       She chants
            'Orneh borneh
            dembeneh korneh
            buckwheat and beans
            dembeh korneh
            oats and black beans:

he who gave you the good eye
from his head his own eyes fly'

or
'In the rafters two cracks lie
in wait to catch the evil eye
Cracks in all the corners lie
in wait to catch the evil eye'

or
'No evil no terror
no wheat and no bran
May Sarah abandon
her crying and pain
Not till the ceiling crops with rye
shall she receive an evil eye'"

H.L. & BARBARA KIRSHENBLATT-GIMBLETT

(Judeo-Arabic, Morocco)
CHILDREN'S RAIN SONGS

1

o the rain drop drop drop drop
o the farmers' little sons
o the landlord Bu-Sukri
o the trip down by the river
o his tumble down the well
o his mother's red tarboosh
o the one-eyed man one-eyed
down the silo in the dark

2

the wind the wind o the bellows
o my uncle o the bellows
it's the blacksmith's bellows
blacksmith gropes his way around

then calls out   children
o my children in the forest
they call   Papa
buy a shirt   or   Papa
buy a black shirt
shirt with carrot-colored sleeves
we eat it all up
whatever there is to eat

J.R.

COMMENTARY

A series of songs sung by children in times of drought. Of other instances of same,
Raphael Patai writes, in *Man & Temple:* "In Morocco the Jews send four children to
the streets to march about holding the four edges of a white linen sheet. The chil-
dren sing: 'The sheaf is thirsty / water it, O Lord!' & the people whom they pass
pour water on the sheet." Similar events are recorded in the Babylonian Talmud,
etc. (For more on Jewish rain-making, see pages 67, 247.)

(Arabic, Yemen)

BRIDE'S SONG AGAINST DEMONS

I
(scenario)

high on a pillow sits with bandaged hands & feet her double sits beside her
dressed like her   large lighted candles   vessels with burning oil
      guard against the demons   on a table stands a basket filled with
eggs & flour   rue is fastened to her headdress

2
(the song)

is mercy's hour now
o devils fade
o devils in the hills of China
diving in its sea

green rue adorns her head
o moon   stretch out
your hands for baubles
for rejoicing   younger days

stretch out your hands for
coloring
the custom of the girls

J.R.

COMMENTARY

"Almost everywhere in the Muslim world, one of the feast days preceding the consummation of a marriage is set aside for the ritual dyeing of the bride's hands & feet with henna. . . . The true aim of the dyeing is probably . . . to protect against the evil eye." (*Encyclopedia of Islam.*)

(Yiddish, traditional)

THE THIEF'S PLAY

ALL   open up   open up
         n lat us in
         we goink to make u heppy here
         if u wimminz shud remember
         what we done for u last year
         now dot it's dis year
         u shud lat us in again

JEW   go lookink around u
         fum all 4 sides
         pretty soon dot tief is
         comink ridink in

THIEF   yas   yas
         I am the thief
         & yer betcher I have cum here
         ter sharpen me old knife

                                        (he stamps his foot)
                o baby I yam one big thief

JEW   (he stamps his foot)
                oy meester u are vun big tief
                                (he pleads)
                so vhy u dunt take
                mine last piece bread
                u shudnt foist kill me
                tief tief tief

THIEF   I don't wantcher
                last piece bread
                but I do want to kill yer
                Jew Jew Jew
                                        (he stamps his foot)
                oh baby I yam one big thief

JEW   (he stamps his foot)
                oy meester u are vun big tief
                                (he pleads)
                so vhy u dunt take
                mine last piece cake
                u shud lat me foist see
                mine dotter married off

THIEF   I dont wantcher
                last piece cake
                & I couldn't care less
                boutcher daughter married off
                                        (he stamps his foot)
                oh baby I yam one big thief

JEW   (he stamps his foot)
                oy meester u are vun big tief
                                (he pleads)
                so vhy u dunt take
                mine last piece fish
                u shud lat me foist give
                to mine fambly ah kiss

THIEF   I dont wantcher

last piece fish
I dont wantcher ter give
yer famly a kiss
                              (he stamps his foot)
oh baby I yam one big thief

JEW   (he stamps his foot)
oy meester u are vun big tief
                    (he pleads)
so vhy u dunt take
mine last liddle piece chicken
u shud lat me foist be
ah fodder by mine children

THIEF   I don't wantcher
last little piece chicken
I don't wantcher ter be
a father to yer children
                              (he stamps his foot)
oh baby I yam one big thief

JEW   (he stamps his foot)
oy meester u are vun big tief
                    (he pleads)
so vhy u dunt take
mine last piece money
u shud lat me foist live
till ah handert mit twanty

THIEF   I dont wantcher
last piece uh money
I dont wantcher ter live
till a hunnert n twunny
                              (he stamps his foot)
oh baby I yam one big thief

JEW   (he stamps his foot)
oy meester u are vun big tief
                    (the thief swats the Jew
                    with his sword & the Jew
                    falls down dead)

                                        J.R.

COMMENTARY

An example of the non-biblical side of the folk theater (i.e., *Purim-shpil*) connected with the Purim holiday as Jewish equivalent to Carnival, etc.

(Yiddish, traditional)

LULLABY A STORY

Once there was a story
The story wasn't feeling happy
The story started out by singing
About a Jewish king

Once there was a king
The king had a queen
The queen had a vineyard
Lullaby the vineyard

The vineyard had a tree
The tree had a branch
The branch had a nest
Lullaby the nest

The nest had a bird
The bird had a wing
The wing had a feather
Lullaby the feather

The king had to die
The queen had to fade away
The tree had a breakdown
The bird vanished from the nest

J.R.

2

Eleazar ha-Kallir (Hebrew, 7th century A.D.)

A CALENDAR: THE YEAR OF THE MESSIAH

---

a

those days: that time:
the first month: NISAN

must surely be the 14th day
o day when Menaḥem ben Ami'el breaks
a path
a way
into Arvel Valley
where his favor burgeons
he will wear the robe of vengeance
as his cloak

b

those days: that time:
the second month: IYAR

hidden dead revealed
among the keepers of
the fallow year
here Korah's band arises
in sight of all the tribes
flies Asaf's banners
from desert sands in Moab
to Acacia's brook

c

those days: that time:
the third month: SIVAN

those who had died in desert
now wake up
great earthquakes overwhelm the walls
while on the mountain's top
corn grows in abundance
earth shaking
the hidden secret told

d

those days: that time:
the fourth month: TAMUZ

fury & rage in all
a king remote from heaven
enters
Old Brute our Enemy will tell him
YOU RIDE FORTH
(relief & rescue only for the few)

e

those days: that time:
the fifth month: AV

this perfect master
cloaked in the robes of vengeance
the Mount of Olives cracked by his rebuke
Messiah now climbs to his fullness
like the sun come forth in fierceness

f

those days: that time:
the sixth month: ELUL

when they see him
the son of Shalti'el
will blow the signal
Mikha'el & Gavri'el descending
the generals of El
propelling vengeance

not leaving life to one last
enemy of El

g

those days: that time:
the seventh month: TISHREI

riots & insurrections
every people
crying
GENOCIDE AGAINST THIS PEOPLE
whom the god of terrors forged
who pulled this people
from within a people
threats to the scorned soul
the hated people

h

those days: that time:
the eighth month: MARHESHVAN

first exile & a storm
blows the Rose back into the desert
where
10,000 will appear
a re-enforcement
last exile how unlike the first

i

those days: that time:
the ninth month: KISLEV

sudden action
sword drops from the sky
blood of the uncircumcised now runs
like streams of water
THE TIME: from three to nine
the One-in-White cries louder
than the cry of water

& the dead rise up & live
"two days after"

j

those days: that time:
the tenth month: TEVET

those fervent each day
each day raise voices
oiiie (they cry) for the changed day
for a famine for 45 days
till they reach his town & praise Yah
each day
each day

k

those days: that time:
the eleventh month: SHEVAT

spasms for 90 thousand
a 100 thousand men in armor
fourth war on the tribal turf of Benjamin
& there
each one of you will chase
a thousand

l

those days: that time:
the twelfth month: ADAR

THREE will be ONE in its rebuilding
the Tishbite & Menaḥem
also Neḥemia
with lovely Tiferet like the priest beside them
& every soul will praise Yah there
AMEN

J.R. / H.L.

COMMENTARY

(1) Like his predecessor, Yannai (below, page 254), Kallir was one of the principal *paytanim* (from the Greek, *poētēs*), makers of a kind of poetry called *piyut:* "compositions added to . . . the ancient prayers [of the synagogue] . . . to constitute – in contrast to the stable and stationary standard prayers – an ever-changing and restless element within the Jewish liturgy . . . that was responsible for the development within medieval Judaism of about half a hundred different rites" (Shalom Spiegel). His work was rediscovered in the 20th century, largely through fragments in the *geniza* (storeroom) of the Cairo Synagogue.

(2) The translation tries to suggest the twists of *piyut* verse-making, while omitting the usual acrostic & end rhyme. An example of high rhyming – sometimes despised by "classicists," etc., but not distant from the "internal" rhyme structurings of Stein, Zukofsky, Duncan, others in our time – is the following *piyut* by Hedvata bar Avraham, circa 10th century, here given as a sound-poem:

A KROVA FOR THE FEAST OF WEEKS

harim alfu zalfu halfu ke-azlu
ba'u meratsdim merakdim mekadedim ve-yagolu
gedura gezura gemura sha'alu
dagar dahar da . . . hallalu
ke-harazta *anokhi* magen – nasim nazolu

nazlu ve-tsiot getsiyot detsiyot nedoney
gavnunim dinunim rinunim megizim mediney
dila gila ila feniney
hushpal hutpal hu'pal ke-meytim ba-anyinei
ke-dibarta matlil *lo yihye nihya mi-pney*

(3) Menahem was a common name for the Messiah; the Tishbite is the prophet Elijah.

(Hebrew, 10th century)

PIYUT: "A GREAT MUSIC"

Ah people do do shake off dust do rise do
Go to Jerusalem see she is praised do
Ride over flagstones break through new roads do
Eat curds eat honey eat up whole rivers do
Add to your stores by their riversides do
Take do plunder the Goyim's prize do
Meet the rays from Shekinah's face do
Use up inherit Jerusalem's fields do
See sun & moon shine their lights do
Illumine with music do sing your songs do
Close with your enemies smoked out burnt off like dew

as written *you have sold yourselves cheap no money can buy all this back*
(J.R., after Isaiah 52.3).

J.R. / H.L.

Samuel ha-Nagid (Hebrew, 993–1056)

THREE LOVE POEMS

I

I'd sell my soul for that fawn
of a boy   night walker
to sound of the 'ud & flute playing
who saw the glass in my hand   said
"drink the wine from between my lips"
& the moon was a *yod* drawn on
the cover of dawn – in gold ink

2

take the blood of the grape from
her red jeweled glass like fire
in middle of hail
this lady with lips of scarlet
thread   roof of her mouth
like good wine
mouth like her body well perfumed:
from blood of corpses the tips
of her fingers are red   thus
half of her hand is like ruby
half quartz

3

that's it – I love that fawn
plucking roses from
your garden –
you can put the blame on me
but if you once looked at my lover
with your eyes
your lovers would be hunting you
& you'd be gone
that boy who told me: pass
some honey from your hive
I answered: give me some back
on your tongue
& he got angry, yelled:
shall we two sin against the living God?
I answered: let your sin,
sweet master, be with me

J.R. / H.L.

Solomon ibn Gabirol (Hebrew, c. 1020–c. 1057)

The 16-Year-Old Poet

I am the prince the song
's my slave   I am the
string all singers songmen
tune   my song's a crown for
kings for ministers a
little crown   am only
sixteen years old but my
heart holds wisdom like some
poet 80 year old man

J.R. / H.L.

Solomon ibn Gabirol (Hebrew, c. 1020–c. 1057)

From Crown of Kingdom   "Constellations"

. . . .

Who can know your ways
making houses for the seven planets within the twelve constellations?
Over Ram and Bull you flowed your strength joining them
the third Twins
two brothers in their unison
the face of them the face of man
and to the fourth the Crab
and to the Lion gave from your glory over
and his sister Virgin next to him
and to the Scales and the Scorpion set by its side
and the ninth made in the form of a hero his strength unfailing
a Bowshot

and so created the Goat and the Pail in your great strength
and by itself the last constellation
Adonai set a great Fish
These are the constellations high and raised in their rising
12 princes to the nations

H.L.

Judah ha-Levi (Hebrew, c. 1075 – c. 1141),
per Charles Reznikoff

From JEHUDA HALEVI'S SONGS TO ZION

My heart in the East
and I at the farthest West:
how can I taste what I eat or find it sweet
while Zion
is in the cords of Edom and I
bound by the Arab?
Beside the dust of Zion
all the good of Spain is light;
and a light thing to leave it.

And if it is now only a land of howling beasts and owls
was it not so
when given to our fathers –
all of it only a heritage of thorns and thistles?
But they walked in it –
His name in their hearts, sustenance! –
as in a park among flowers.

In the midst of the sea
when the hills of it slide and sink
and the wind
lifts the water like sheaves –
now a heap of sheaves and then a floor for the threshing –
and sail and planks shake
and the hands of the sailors are rags,

and no place for flight but the sea,
and the ship is hidden in waves
like a theft in the thief's hand,
suddenly the sea is smooth
and the stars shine on the water.

Wisdom and knowledge – except to swim –
have neither fame nor favor here;
a prisoner of hope, he gave his spirit to the winds,
and is owned by the sea;
between him and death – a board.

Zion, do you ask if the captives are at peace –
the few that are left?
I cry out like the jackals when I think of their grief;
but, dreaming of the end of their captivity,
I am like a harp for your songs.

Abraham ibn Ezra (Hebrew, 1089 – 1164)

"I HAVE A GARMENT"

I have a garment which is like a sieve
Through which girls sift barley and wheat.
In the dead of night I spread it out like a tent
And a thousand stars pierce it with their gleams.
Sitting inside, I see the moon and the Pleiades
And on a good night, the great Orion himself.
I get awfully tired of counting all the holes
Which seem to me like the teeth of many saws.
A piece of thread to sew up all the other threads
Would be, to say the least, superfluous.
If a fly landed on it with all his weight,
The little idiot would hang by his foot, cursing.
Dear God, do what you can to mend it.
Make me a mantle of praise from these poor rags.

ROBERT MEZEY

Isaac ben Abraham Gorni (Hebrew, 13th century)
PROENSA

In Provence Gorni's got a lot of enemies
who put down my songs as well.
Yet I know I am the poet,
the only one of my generation.
When I sing mountains dance
valleys & forests rejoice.
I take up my harp & happy
Zion's daughters form a circle.
If I want I can wake up bones
& make stones run like the Jordan.

. . . .

When I die girls will lament me everyday
& merchants make big deals in world-markets
for bags of dirt from my grave, out of my coffin's
planks others will carve amulets – special for barren women.
Someone will string harps & fiddles
with my hair & the tunes will come, O
lovely tunes sans strum or bow of human hand.
Even my clothes – revered – anything that's touched my skin.
        But grind my bones to dust,
        I won't promote idolatry.

GEORGE ECONOMOU

Immanuel ben Solomon of Rome (Italian, c. 1261–after 1328)

ITALIAN SONNET

Love knows neither law nor
rule, is deaf & blind to them,
admits no impediments. Love's
strength cannot be measured or
his will opposed. Love runs
the world, fills this earth and
neither *pater noster* nor any
other rite or charm will work.
Nobody puts down his pride
or turns off his power. No-
body slips out of Amor's
wide nets, and to all my
petitions the same old answer:
"That's the way I want it!"

GEORGE ECONOMOU

Kalonymos ben Kalonymos (Hebrew, 1286–after 1328)

From STONE OF CHOICE

Damn the one damn
Let his tongue split
Spit on the one
The onanist who gave
My father the "good" news:
You have a son!
Pity the fathers, yes,
And the mothers

Who have male children.
What a joke!
And what a terrible burden.
Armies, armies of prohibitions
And commandments lie in wait,
Positive, negative, and eternal
Who can fulfill these obligations?
No matter how responsible he is
Who can fulfill 613 commandments?
Who can do it?
It's impossible.
I'm a sinner and a lawbreaker.

It would have been wonderful
To have been born a girl – with flowing
Hair and green eyes
And be expert at a spinning wheel
Or crocheting with my friends.
During dusktime, the girls and I
Would drink coffee and
Eat cookies, telling stories,
Planning shopping trips to the city
Etc.
People would be impressed
At my talent for crocheting
I'd create the loveliest patterns!
Then at the appropriate time
I'd marry a beautiful youth
How he would adore me
We would touch each other everywhere.
His gifts, gold and diamonds,
Would adorn me
And he'd carry me around on his hands
Kissing and hugging me.

But my fate
The bitterness of it!
I was born a man
So God willed it.
I can't be changed.
I can't be changed
From a man into a woman.

I will accept it in love
And thank the Holy One, blessed be He,
With the words:
"Blessed art thou, Lord, who has
Not made me a woman."

ROCHELLE OWENS

Maulana Sahin (Judeo-Persian, 14th century)

From THE EPIC OF KING KISHVAR   "The Castle"

---

high & green
was like the moon's face
he had placed
into the rose garden
4 gates opened on
its flowers
where the vizier stood
suddenly
the sky would strut up
to the king:
a circle
center of the castle
with a marble basin
held no pebbles
but rubies   jewels
& a hollow column
a golden peacock
stood on
spun around
poured water from its beak
the fountain filled
the king was like a rose

held wine in hand
or like narcissus drank

. . . .

& told the cup-bearer
to fill
the bowl with veils
the bearer (body
like a rose)
poured red into the bowl
a golden bird
at center
musk & ambergris
the king would raise it
to his mouth
(o roses)
& the bird called: drink
he kissed the earth
bowed down
the great king took
a hit of wine
drawn from the moon

                                                        J.R.

Israel ben Moses Najara (Hebrew, c. 1555 – 1628)
"Children of the Times"

Children of the times are vines
    Death the vintner gathers,
            as he pleases beneath the Creator's eyes –

            carefully gathers the grapes –
bud and seed,
        old man, suckling infant,
    beggar, prince,

the great and noble together with
the despicable poor
and there's no one he misses.

With a deaf ear for the cries of the transitory
and a silver indifference
that grinds ore back to dust.

And if the intelligent ones put in for their last supplies,
he quashes that temporal lust,
scythes through the sprouts,
strives for perfection,
finishes off the soul,
for no Power, no Cunning,
can defend against the Lord.

JACK HIRSCHMAN

THE END OF "A BOOK OF WRITINGS"

A Book of Extensions

Abraham Abulafia (Hebrew, 1240–c. 1291)

From THE BOOK OF THE LETTER

. . . . . .

       And Adonai said to
     Zechariahu the Messenger,
      Raise your voice
        with the tongue
           of your pen,
     write
the word of God, this book with
your three
fingers; and God was
with him as guide, and he wrote
all that was commanded
and he came reciting the words
of God to the Jews circumcised
in the flesh as well as the
dullheaded and poor, but
they paid no heed to the form
of his coming, spoke of him
and his god in unimaginable
terms

JACK HIRSCHMAN

(Greek, before 6th Century A.D.)

A PERFORMANCE ON THE GREAT NAME FROM
THE EIGHTH OR HIDDEN SACRED BOOK OF MOSES
CALLED "UNIQUE" OR "HOLY"

The instruction: Speaking to the rising sun, stretching out your right hand to the left and your left hand / likewise to the left, say "A." To the north, putting forward only your right fist, say "E." Then to the west, extending both hands in front [of you], say "Ē." To the south, / [holding] both on your stomach, say, "I." To the earth, bending over, touching the ends of your toes, say "O." Looking into the air, having your hand on your heart, say "Y." Looking in the sky, having both hands on your head, say "Ō:"

	sky	
A	Ō Ō Ō Ō Ō Ō Ō	IIII
east	Ō Ō Ō Ō Ō Ō O	south
air	y y y y y y	
north	e e o o o o o Ē Ē Ē	west
	earth	

I call on you, eternal and unbegotten, who are one, who alone hold together the whole creation of all things, whom none understands, whom the gods worship, / whose name not even the gods can utter. Inspire from your exhalation (?), ruler of the pole, him who is under you; accomplish for me the NN thing.

"I call on you as by the voice of the male gods, IĒŌ OYE ŌĒI YE AŌ EI ŌY AOĒ OYĒ / EŌA YĒI ŌEA OĒŌ IEOU AŌ. I call on you, as by the voice of the female gods, IAĒ EŌO IOY EĒI ŌA EĒ IĒ AI YO ĒIAY EŌO OYĒE IAŌ ŌAI EOYĒ YŌĒI IŌA. I call on you, as the winds / call you. I call on you, as the dawn." (Looking toward dawn [say], "A EE ĒĒĒ IIII OOOOO YYYYY ŌŌŌŌŌŌŌ.") "I call on you as the south." (Looking to the south say, "I OO YYY ŌŌŌŌ AAAAA EEEEE ĒĒĒĒĒĒ.") / "I call on you as the west." (Standing [facing] the west, say, "E II OOO YYYY ŌŌŌŌŌ AAAAAA EEEEEE.") "I call on you as the north." (Standing looking toward the north say, "Ō AA EEE ĒĒĒĒ IIIII

OOOOOO YYYYYY.") "I call on you / as the earth." (Looking toward
the earth say, "E ĒĒ III OOOO YYYYY ŌŌŌŌŌŌ AAAAAAA.") "I call
on you as the sky." (Looking into the sky say, "Y ŌŌ AAA EEEE ĒĒĒĒĒ
IIIIII OOOOOOO.") "I call on you as the cosmos, O YY ŌŌŌ AAAA /
EEEEE ĒĒĒĒĒĒ IIIIIII. I call on your name, the greatest among gods. If
I say it complete, there will be an earthquake, the sun will stop and the
moon will be afraid and the rocks and the mountains and the sea and the
rivers / and every liquid will be petrified; the whole cosmos will be thrown
into confusion. I call on you, IYEYO ŌAEĒ IAŌ AEĒ AI EĒ AĒ IOYŌ
EYĒ IEOU AĒŌ ĒI ŌĒI IAĒ IŌOYĒ AYĒ YĒA IŌ IŌAI IŌAI ŌĒ /
EE OY IŌ IAŌ, the great name. Become for me lynx, eagle, snake, phoe-
nix, life, power, necessity, images of god, AIŌ IŌY IAŌ ĒIŌ AA OYI
AAAA E IY IŌ ŌĒ IAŌ AI AŌĒ OYEŌ AIEĒ IOYE YEIA EIŌ ĒII
YY EE ĒĒ ŌĀOĒ / CHECHAMPSIMM CHANGALAS EĒIOY IĒEA
ŌOĒOE (seven of the auspicious [names?]) ZŌIŌIĒR ŌMYRYROM-
ROMOS." [Say it?] thus, extending the second AIŌ: "Ē II YY ĒĒ
OAOĒ."
This initiation is performed to the suns of the thirteenth day of the
month, when the gold lamella is licked / off and one says over it: "IAIA IY
OĒ IEYOŌ ĒŌI EO Ē ŌY EĒ YŌĒ ŌŌO ŌŌI ŌAŌ EŌ OĒ YŌ." Then
more completely, "AŌEYĒ OAI IO ĒYEŌA OYŌ ŌO EI OY ĒO OIYY
ŌYY ŌI A / EE ĒĒĒ IIII OOOOO YYYYY ŌŌŌŌŌŌ AŌ EOĒ
EŌĒ IAA ĒŌI ĒIŌ. In [the] initiation these things are said six times with
all [the rest?], and the seven vowels are written on the gold lamella to be
licked off, and on the silver lamella the seven vowels for the phylactery /
OĒŌ AŌ OOO YOIĒ OY YĒI SORRA THŌŌM CHRALAMPĒAPS
ATOYĒGI. The following series of vowels [are written as] "wings"; and on
the gold lamella write this AŌEYĒOI; on the silver: IOĒYEŌA, . . .

AEĒIOYŌ	AEĒIOYŌŌ	AEĒIOYŌOYŌ
EĒIOYŌA	EĒIOYŌŌA	EĒIOYŌOYŌA
ĒIOYŌAE	ĒIOYŌŌAE	ĒIOYŌOYŌAE
IOYŌAEĒ	IOYŌŌAEĒ	IOYŌOYŌAEĒ
OYŌAEĒI	OYŌŌAEĒI	OYŌOYŌAEĒI
YŌAEĒIO	YŌŌAEĒIO	YŌOYŌAEĒIO
ŌAEĒIOY	ŌŌAEĒIOY	ŌOYŌAEĒIOY

and the great heaven, eternal, incorruptible, OEŌ AŌ THOOU OIĒ OY
YĒI ORCHRA THŌŌMCHRA SEMESILAMPS / ATOYĒTI DROU-
SOUAR DROUĒSRŌ GNIDA BATAIANA ANGASTA AMASOUR-
OUR OUANA APAISTOU OUANDA ŌTI SATRAPERKMĒPH ALA
Dionysus, blessed EYIE YOY YYY THENŌR conducting YYY EYE-

YEY YE OYŌ XERTHENATHIA THAPHTHŌ / OIKROU ŌR ARAX
GŌ Ō AAA ERARĒRAYIIĒR THOUTH ASĒSENACHTHŌ
LARNIBAI AIOŌ KOUPHIŌ ISŌTHŌNI PATHENI IEEENTHĒR
PANCHOCHITAS OYE TIASOUTH PACHTHEESTH HYSEM-
MIGADŌN / ORTHŌ BAUBŌ NOĒRADĒR SOIRE SOIRE
SANKANTHARA ERESCHIGAL APARA KEŌPH IAŌ SABAŌTH
ABRATIAŌTH ADŌNAI ZAGOURĒ HARSAMOSI RANAKER-
NŌTH LAMPSOUŌR. Therefore, I am brought together with you by the
great commander-in-chief Michael, lord, the great archangel of IEOY AĒ
AIŌ EYAI / I Ē IĒ IŌA IĒIĒ AIŌ EĒ AIŌ. Therefore, I am conjoined
[with you], O great one, and I have you in my heart AŌ EĒ EŌĒI AIAĒ ŌĒ
IŌAŌ EOĒE ŌĒI AAĒ ŌĒIŌ.

HANS DITER BETZ

COMMENTARY

(1) From Greek magical papyrus – attributed to Jewish sources – in which the
magic is carried by the voiced breath: a combination & recombination of vowels,
also used in naming. The Roman letters (original: Greek) permit the writing down
or stabilization of the vowels, which would be part of the *oral* tradition in Hebrew,
where only consonants are written down. Thus, until the masoretic vocalizations
(circa 6th – 7th centuries A.D.) there was no fixed Hebrew text that could be read
without the oral transmission of soundings. In the papyrus, above, the directions for
transformation of text to sound are evident – along with the attendant movements.
Viewed in this light they offer the remains of what Dada poets & others in our cen-
tury re-invented as the "sound-poem": patterns of "abstract" sound intended to be
read aloud. Wrote Hugo Ball of his own first soundings (1915): "I now noticed that
my voice, which seemed to have no other choice, had assumed the age-old cadence
of the sacerdotal lamentation."

Compare Malinowski on Trobriand Island "garden magic": "The magic is in the
breath, & the breath is the magic."

(2) "God said to Moses, 'I will make you write most of my Torah but not all' . . .
because the oral transmission is the mystery of God, & God hands over his
mysteries only to the righteous." (From *Midrash Tanḥuma* 6.)

Isaac the Blind (Hebrew, c. 1325)

LOCK YOUR HEART THAT IT MAY NOT BROOD
                                                    Sefer Yetsira, 1.8

That we may not brood – concerning that which is hidden to thought,
lest we fall into confusion.   For only from that which we comprehend

are we able to recognize also that which we cannot comprehend.
& to that end word-spheres arose.

For language comprehends
only that out of which it comes

                    since humanity is unable to grasp
                    the word of the divine,

                    & the letters of the alphabet,
                    but only the word of language itself.

& there are no words
outside the letters of the alphabet.
                    & all the divine words are given
                    to be meditated upon.

                    For all spheres fill themselves up
                    from a sphere above

                    & they are given in order
                    to meditate from the sphere-word that appears

                    in your heart,
                    to meditate

                    up to the infinite.

For there is no path to prayer
other than that whereby

humanity is sucked up by finite words
& rises in thinking to the infinite.

GARY G. GACH

Moses Cordovero (Hebrew, 1522–70)

From THE GARDEN OF POMEGRANATES

"The Unity of God"

י = Y (yod)
ה = H (hey)
ו = V (vav)
א = alef = one

(Samaritan Hebrew, traditional)

CONCRETE POEM: "YHVH GREAT GOD"

```
Y  H  V  H  G  R  E  A  T  G  O  D  Y
H  V  H  G  R  E  A  T  G  O  D  Y  H
V  H  G  R  E  A  T  G  O  D  Y  H  V
H  G  R  E  A  T  G  O  D  Y  H  V  H
G  R  E  A  T  G  O  D  Y  H  V  H  G
R  E  A  T  G  O  D  Y  H  V  H  G  R
E  A  T  G  O  D  Y  H  V  H  G  R  E
A  T  G  O  D  Y  H  V  H  G  R  E  A
T  G  O  D  Y  H  V  H  G  R  E  A  T
G  O  D  Y  H  V  H  G  R  E  A  T  G
O  D  Y  H  V  H  G  R  E  A  T  G  O
D  Y  H  V  H  G  R  E  A  T  G  O  D
```

J.R.

Moses Cordovero (Hebrew, 1522–70)

COMPOSITION AROUND THE INEFFABLE NAME

(the topmost line): "... He will bring us to the time when Earth is filled with knowledge of the Name. Amen Amen. The Name be blest forever. Amen Amen."
(the inner circle): Y-H-V-H (the tetragrammaton) in the center surrounded by its permutations in four groups of six pairs.
(outside the inner circle): [1] beginning with the larger word, הנה, & working outwards & counterclockwise, the two circular lines concern the transmutations of Y-H-V-H, linked (through gematria?) with the three initial words of the Priestly Blessing, *yevarekhekha*, *ya'er* & *yisa* (all of which are followed by the tetragrammaton in the blessing itself), & with the phrases, *midat yom* (aspect of day / maleness) & *midat layla* (aspect of night / femaleness); [2] block letters are the initial words of the Priestly Blessing (see above) intermixed with the letters of the tetragrammaton; beneath the first block letters are transmutations of the tetragrammaton, & under the second block letters is the name of "72" (see below, page 219) in twelve groups of six three-letter syllables.

NAME EVENT ONE

Slice an apple in three.
Write a name on each slice & eat it.

NAME EVENT TWO

Write a name in the sand.
Have participants lick it up.

Abraham Abulafia (Hebrew, 1240–c. 1291)

From LIFE OF THE WORLD TO COME   "Circles"

(I)

מערכה ראשונה

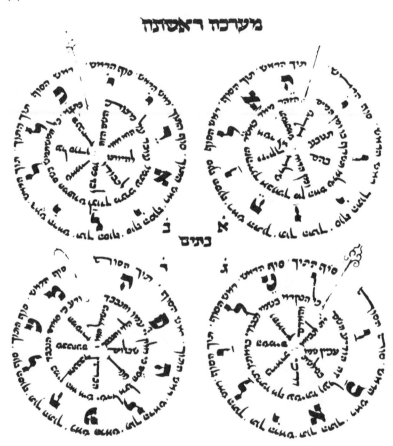

נתים

READING INSTRUCTIONS: Beginning at the marker: the outer rims read right to left; the inner rim leads to the inner spokes, & from circle into circle, right to left. The words at top = "first order."

UPPER RIGHT

outer rim: middle of the first . middle of the last . first of the last . last of the last . first of the middle . middle of the middle . last of the middle . first of the first . last of the first

middle rim (large letters): permutations of the name "72"

inner rim: **be very wary as your fathers warned you of the fire don't be burnt by it & water**

inner spokes: **not to / drown / in it / & wind / that it not / harm you / you not / use**

UPPER LEFT

outer rim: first of the last . middle of the middle . middle of the first . first of the first . middle of the last . last of the last . first of the middle . last of the middle . first of the first . last of the first

middle rim (large letters): permutations of the name "72"

inner rim: **it on condition anyone who takes the name for his own needs transgresses the command**

inner spokes: **about said name / was formed / to be / for his own glory / only thus / the prophet / said about / its secret**

LOWER RIGHT

outer rim: last of the middle . last of the first . first of the last . middle of the last . first of the middle . middle of the first . middle of the middle . first of the first . last of the last

middle rim (large letters): permutations of the name "72"

inner rim: **whatever has my name I made it for my honor formed it worked it truly & concerning this the name informed**

inner spokes: **his prophets (be he blest) / about his name / by 3 / ways / of creation/ of the skies / & earth / & man**

LOWER LEFT

outer rim: last of the first . last of the middle . last of the last . middle of the middle . first of the first . middle of the first . first of the middle . first of the last . middle of the last

middle rim (large letters): permutations of the name "72"

inner rim: **& know according to the name the one most honored is the one of Israel because the name's own portion is his people & the most honored one**

inner spokes: **of Israel is / the Levite & the most honored / of the Levites / is the / priest / & the most honored / of the priests / is the Messiah**

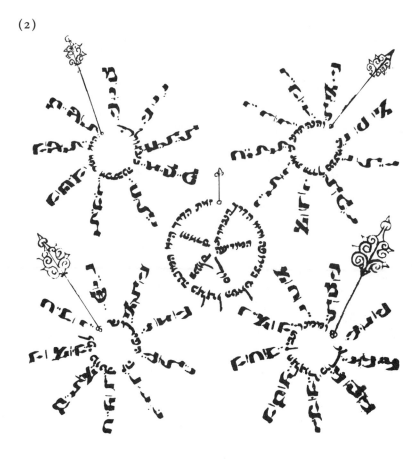

READING INSTRUCTIONS: Right to left & circle into circle toward the center. Larger letters are permutations of the name "72."

UPPER RIGHT, *the rim:* o look here now this is the way itself

UPPER LEFT, *the rim:* by which you'll understand the gilgul metempsychosis complete

LOWER RIGHT, *the rim:* the one I now write in the circle

LOWER LEFT, *the rim:* the intention of the explanation

CENTER, *the rim:* way that may be understood as three-fold gilgul metempsychosis

CENTER, *the spokes:* the chosen way / disclosing / secrets / of the world / & man

(3)

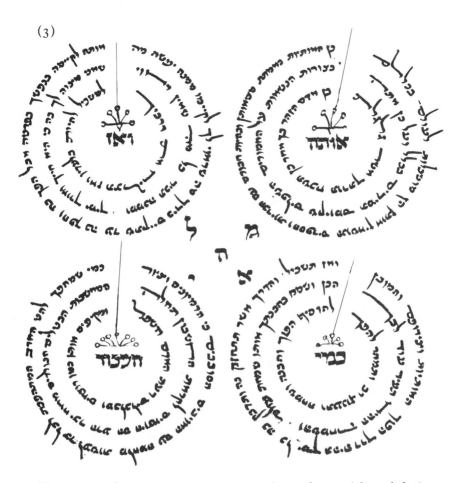

READING INSTRUCTIONS: upper rims to lower, right to left, & circle into circle.

UPPER RIGHT

so are the letters in their true essentials & when joined to people & to books that carry them are made intelligible as wholes to world & public: forms that the lowly asses carry though their existence is eternal: so then manchild you be careful that you not forget that you are working transformation of the Torah

UPPER LEFT

making it exist inside your soul in its particulars: so turn through it o turn through it & what of it is fit for your fulfillment let your hand fulfill: do what I tell you here it is your life your length of days from which you come to know what isn't fitting that a wise man be without & then your ways will be successful

& then you will be wise: the way that you must cleave to & be strong in all your days will be the way of turning letters & combining them: & understanding what is understood rejoicing in your understandings & eternally rejoicing this rejoicing further wakening your heart to keep on turning them & understanding: joy & pleasures as you rush to turn

LOWER LEFT

like one who turns the sword the flame that turns itself toward every side & wages war against the enemies around you: for the empty images & forms of thought born of the evil impulse are the first emerging into thought surrounding it like murderers to foul the gnosis of the lowly tortured man

·

· ·

& the secret

ITS MEASURE IS RIGHT	& LEFT
MEASURE OF ITS RIGHT	ITS LEFT
MEASURE OF ITS LEFT	ITS RIGHT
IT HAS NO IMAGE	SKIES
IMAGE OF ITS RIGHT	LEFT
IMAGE OF ITS LEFT	RIGHT
& ITS BIRTHPLACE	BEING FROM NON-BEING
FATHERING FROM NOTHING	NAMES

·

· ·

MY NAME IS OTHER THAN	
WHAT HAS NO	IMAGE
MY IMAGE IS OTHER THAN	
WHAT HAS NO	NAME
& I HAVE NO NAME	OTHER THAN IMAGE
& I HAVE NO IMAGE	OTHER THAN NAME
EN-EY-EM-EE	WRITTEN OUT FULLY
MY NAME AN IMAGINING	FOR MY TRUTH

J.R. / H.L.

(1) Abulafia's poetry of permutations (a kind of medieval "lettrism," etc.) here takes the form of nearly 200 circles, consisting of a discourse on meditation, a set of instructions for specific permutations, & the permutations of the letters themselves. In the present instance the permutations work off the so-called Name-of-72: i.e., 72 three-letter syllables "based on the three verses of Exodus 14.19 – .21, each of which contains 72 letters. . . . [It] was made up by joining the first letter of verse 19, the last letter of 20, and the first of 21, to form its first triad; the second letter of 19, the penultimate of 20, and the second of 21, to make the second triad, and so on until we have 72 three-letter terms comprising all the letters of these verses." (J. Trachtenberg, *Jewish Magic & Superstition*, page 94.) Abulafia in turn arranges the syllables in rows & columns, then sets them into circles according to instructions ("middle of the first, middle of the last," etc.), which form part of the circles as well. In this way the disciple is led into the circles, must follow their message as an act of concentration.

Abulafia himself writes of the abstracting/spiritualizing process which he then employs & by which the world is apprehended as language/sound: "Know that the method of *tseruf* (the combination of letters) can be compared to music; for the ear hears sounds from various combinations, in accordance with the character of the melody & the instrument. Also, two different instruments can form a combination, & if the sounds combine, the listener's ear registers a pleasant sensation in acknowledging their difference. . . . The same is true of the combination of letters. It touches the first string, which is comparable to the first letters, & proceeds to the second, third, fourth, & fifth, & the various sounds combine. And the secrets, which express themselves in these combinations, delight the heart which acknowledges its God & is filled with ever fresh joy." Thus the letters – by a process called *dilug* (skipping) – become a basis for meditation "on the essence of one's thought, abstracting from it every word, be it connected with a notion or not . . . (by putting) the consonants which one is combining into swift motion." (From *Sha'are Tsedek*, for which, see G. Scholem, *Major Trends in Jewish Mysticism*, pages 154 – 55.) For Abulafia & others, such processes remain essentially "oral," in the sense of openended: an improvisatory meditation on a fixed base (torah, names of God, etc.) whose true meanings are not "literal" but the occasion for an ongoing process of reconstruction (revelation) & sounding. In touch with Yogic currents from the East, Abulafia's intention here seems clearly mantric; but his practice of a systemic & concrete poetry also closely resembles the 20th-century lettrism of Isidore Isou, the asymmetries & nuclei of Jackson Mac Low, & the blues kabbala improvisations of Jack Hirschman, all of whom he may have influenced.

(2) "Abulafia who was never admitted into the great rabbinic canon of the Jews because in fact   he was the Jews first truly modern poet / visual artist   saw the abstract musical beauty of the letters   of the Hebrew alphabet   went for the form of the thing itself   which of course was nothing   but the absolute *ain* of the pinpointed pain   of the elohimic struggle." (J. Hirschman.)

Wallace Berman (1926–76)

From IMAGE OF THE WALL

(Hebrew, medieval)

THE MASORA CALLIGRAMS

1) "DOG & HARE"

2) "JONAH"

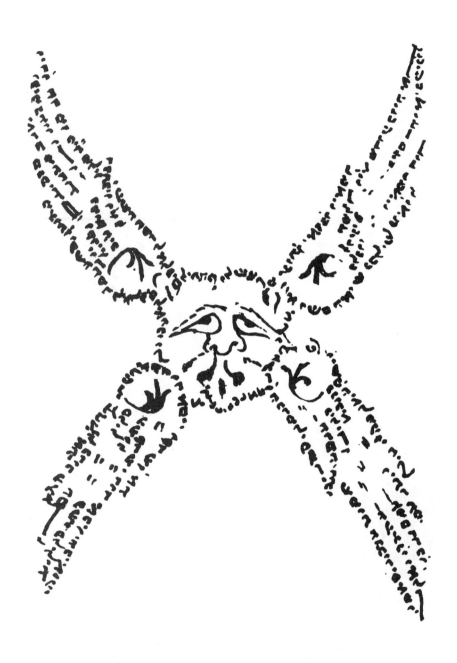

Words drawn into visual images have a near universal distribution among cultures that practice writing—more elaborate & expansive, less literal & literary than the "shaped poems" per George Herbert, etc., would lead us to believe. In Apollinaire's *Calligrammes* (circa 1914), the mode is revived—& re-shaped, smashed open—with the claim, e.g., in his "horse calligram": "You will find here a new representation of the universe. The most poetic & the most modern."

The masora "calligrams" occur here & there in traditional annotated copies of the Hebrew Bible. Writes Berjouhi Bowler (*The Word As Image*, page 128): "In some Hebrew manuscripts the massorah, which is the critical emendation found [as marginalia] on certain pages of the Bible, ceases to be the usual three lines, in minuscule letters, surrounding the biblical text. Unexpectedly . . . the massorah is shaped into patterns which generally have no particular relevance to the biblical passage or to the emendations and alternative readings [that make up their text]. The strange intrusions can appear either as a full page decoration . . . or in corners of the page. There is no apparent reason for their appearance."

Those reproduced here are in minute writing & have been greatly enlarged. Although the scribes' disregard of injunctions against iconography, etc., is obvious, the intention is otherwise unknown. Thus, Bowler again: "As the massorah proceeded, it became extremely abstruse and less understood. . . . Written by mere men to clarify the revelation of God, to safeguard the Word from the abuse of mortality and change, [the massorah] itself became the mystery. The mystery grows denser as the words themselves are swirled into these elaborate decorations. . . . As the rational content vanishes, a new communication occurs. The forms grow into these archetypal shapes and appear before us. We are invited to drop for an instant our existential alienation and join the dance." ("The Word As Ikon," *Typographica* 8, London, 1968.)

Compare the Tzara calligram which follows.

Tristan Tzara (French 1896–1963)

Calligram

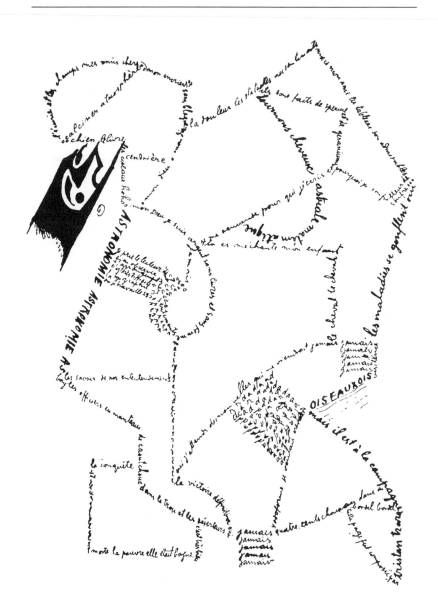

Jacques Gaffarel (17th century)

CELESTIAL ALPHABET EVENT

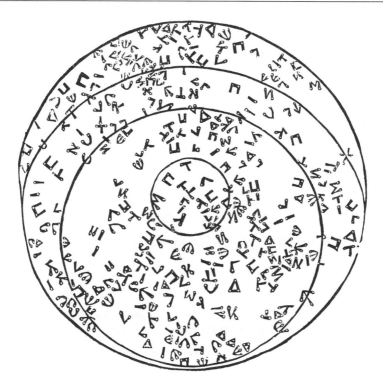

COMMENTARY

(1) An extreme example of a language process event based on natural phenomena, this derives from Hebrew alphabetic practice projected on the night sky. The key is calligraphic: a form of the alphabet ("magic letters") going back to Hellenistic period, in which the lines of the letters culminate in rounded points (thus,

א, alef, = ✕), permitting a later application to the night sky, where patterns of

stars (points joined by "lines") can then be read as letters, groups of letters read as words, etc. In the process the sky becomes a massive concrete poem, whose words or "messages" are constantly transforming. The instance, above, is from Jacques Gaffarel, a Christian kabbalist of the 17th century, but the viability of the process is dependent on the Hebrew alphabet, where the absence of explicit vowels allows a wide range of meaningful readings.

(2) "To the realm of practical Kabbalah ... belong the many traditions concerning the existence of a special archangelic alphabet, the earliest of which was 'the alphabet of Metatron.' Other such alphabets of *kolmosin* ('[angelic] pens') were attributed to Michael, Gabriel, Raphael, etc. Several of these alphabets that have come down to us resemble cuneiform writing, while some clearly derive from early Hebrew or Samaritan script. In kabbalistic literature they are known as 'eye writing' (*ketav einayim*) because their letters are always composed of lines and small circles that resemble eyes." (G. Scholem, *Kabbalah*, page 186.)

(3) Says the *Zohar:* "He who travels in the early morning shall look carefully to the east. He will see there something like letters marching in the sky, some rising, others descending. These brilliant characters are the letters with which God has formed heaven & earth." Read alternatively as numbers, they recall the Pythagoreans' vision of the sky set down by Aristotle: "They supposed the elements of number to be the elements of all things, & the whole heaven to be a musical scale [harmonia] & number." (*Metaphysics* 985b.)

Moses Cordovero (Hebrew, 1522–70)

The 10 Sefirot As a Labyrinth of Letters

Depiction of the *sefirot* as stages of God's immanence (see above, page 24) has taken a variety of forms: e.g., as tree, as human body, as hand, as wheel of light, etc. Here Cordovero works off the initial letters of the *sefirot*, formalizing these into a maze pattern, with the initial letter of the tenth & closest *sefira – mem = malkhut* (= kingdom = shekinah) – in familiar form at center. The Hebrew letters throughout represent numbers as well as sounds (see below, page 232) – thus lead the way into a poetry of numbers, itself presented in a variety of modes.

Maria Hebrea (1st century B.C.)

THE NUMBERS

---

2 are 1
3 & 4 are 1
1 will become 2
2 will become 3

COMMENTARY

The entry through alchemy, in the figure of Mary the Jewess, said by some to be the mother of the art. Of her verbalizations only these formulas survive, reminiscent of e. e. cummings' description of the poet's strategy: to hold that 2 times 2 *is 5*. Or Edmond Jabès of a *poesis* specifically Jewish: "The number '4,' he said, is the number of our ruin. Do not think I am mad. The number '4' equals 2 times 2. It is in the name of such obsolete logic that we are persecuted. For we hold that 2 times 2 equals also 5, or 7, or 9. You only need to consult the commentaries of our sages to verify. Not everything is simple in simplicity. We are hated because we do not enter into the simple calculations of mathematics." (*The Book of Questions,* page 92.)

It is at some such point that the equation by the Russian poet Marina Tsvetayeva – that "all poets are Jews" – reveals its meaning.

(Medieval, anonymous)

A TALISMAN FOR VENUS

22	47	16	41	10	35	4
5	23	48	17	42	11	29
30	6	24	49	18	36	12
13	21	7	25	43	19	37
38	14	32	1	26	44	30
21	39	8	33	2	27	45
46	15	40	9	34	3	28

COMMENTARY

(1) "The total of the numbers is equal to the value – in letters – of the number [name] of the intelligence [guardian spirit] of Venus. The talisman is drawn on copper, the metal of the planet, and is used for operations in which spirits connected with this planet are invoked." (Idries Shah, *The Secret Lore of Magic.*) The columns & lines equal 175 in all directions.

(2) Once viewed as aberrant, etc., forms like these can now be seen as more central, even centrally human. Writes Eric Mottram of "neo-Pythagorean arithmology" from Middle Ages to Mac Low: "Numerology assumes a universal unity, which can be drawn upon for limitations of nature; so that creation is a part of Creation, whether issued from an Author or made by an author in the image of universal authority. The poetry of numerology is part of the long dialectic of freedom and necessity, of the human search for a vocabulary and syntax through which to explore and limit. . . . There is nothing slavish, degrading or anti-human in it, unless used as a limited imposition of geometry as the model of a State. Anarchism balances between chance and necessity, as nature does. The totalitarian state, simply, is not total but partial, an imposition of insane reason." (From "Compositions of the Magus: The Art of Jackson Mac Low," in *Vort* 8.) At least "numbers" – a traditional term for metrics, poetry, etc. – is seen in its full extent & tied at origin to an attempt to form a viable, transforming image of the real world.

(3) An extensive Jewish presence behind medieval magic, often invoked in texts like these by names like Moses, Solomon, etc. Part of the image of the Jew as magician *par excellence*, the dangerous possessor of occulted powers.

Charlie Morrow (b. 1942)

A NUMBER BLESSING

1.	B	1.	B	
2.	A	1.2.	BA	
3.	R	1.2.3.	BAR	
4.	U	1.2.3.4.	BARU	
5.	CH	1.2.3.4.5.	BARUCH	

```
12345   BARUCH
12345   BARUCH
12345   BARUCH
12345   BARUCH
12345   BARUCH

12341   BARU B
12341   BARU B
12341   BARU B
12341   BARU B
12341   BARU B

12311   BAR BB
12311   BAR BB
12311   BAR BB
12311   BAR BB
12311   BAR BB

12111   BA BBB
12111   BA BBB
12111   BA BBB
12111   BA BBB
12111   BA BBB

11111   BBBBB
11111   BBBBB
11111   BBBBB
11111   BBBBB
11111   BBBBB
```

1975

COMMENTARY

"Counting is a way of labeling pulses. Simple counting takes a calm, even tone of voice, a scientific tone – the cantillation of facts, facts by themselves – a list of the names of distances, a set of regular guideposts, equidistant.

"For a musician, counting is part of the job. Music is measured, and these measures are felt against a matrix of pulses.

"... Hanging numbers like signposts on locations, as in the performance of my counts with complex sound systems or several counters, is a meditative geometry.

"... The numbers may be read on one tone or associated with pitches, in scaleform or any form. They can be played on instruments.

"In the number blessing the word B A R U C H (Hebrew: "blessed") is meant to be sung in the traditional ascending fourth.

"... The space implied by the end of a line and the beginning of the next line should be dealt with consistently within any particular performance. It can be said of the number pieces, that it is the consistency of their realization that is special about them." (Charlie Morrow.)

---

25 GEMATRIA

Light
A mystery.

Eye
Silver.

The Upper World
Is all the chariot

He & He
This & this.

Metatron
The beard.
The beard.

Messenger
Five.

The Witness
A jewel.

The Body
The reward.

The World / The Year / The Soul
Evening.
Morning.
Noon.

First Adam
Hell is open.

Moses
I am.
I am.
I am.

The Garden
Shadow.
Stone.
The Brain.

The Soul of Adam
Lilith.

Israel
El Song.

Rebekka
This.
12.

The River
The prayerbook.

Incense
The ark.
613.

Wisdom
Is.
Was.
Will be.

Messiah
Snake.

The Devil
Fat-ash.

This Pope
This garbage.

Dominus
Demonus.

Money
The tree.

"& the king said

to Haman: the
money will be
yours"

Death
903.

Israel Alone
Therefore.

J.R. / H.L.

COMMENTARY

Gematria is the general term for a variety of traditional coding practices used to establish correspondences between words or series of words based on the numerical equivalence of the sums of their letters or on the interchange of letters according to a set system. The numerical method – *gematria* per se – typically took *alef* as 1, *bet* as 2, *yod* as 10, *kuf* as 100, etc., through *tav* (last letter) as 400 – although more complicated methods (e.g., reduction to single digits, etc.) were later introduced. Non-numerical methods included (1) anagrams, or rearrangements of the letters of a word to form a new word or word series, as "god" or "dog" in English; (2) *notarikon*, the derivation of a new word from the initial letters of several others & vice versa, as "god," say from "garden of delight"; & (3) *temura*, various systems of letter code, e.g., the common one in which the first half of the alphabet is placed over the second & letters are substituted between the resultant rows, etc., *in search of meaningful combinations.*

   Processes of this kind go back to Greek, even Babylonian, practice, & early enter the rabbinic literature. But the greatest development was among kabbalists from the 12th century on, who used it both to discover divine & angelic names & to uncover correspondences between ideas & images by means free of subjective interference. When set out as poems, the resemblance of the *gematria* to a poetry of correspondences in our own time is evident, as also to instances of process poetry & art based on (more or less) mechanical formulas for the generation of both simple & extended series of permutations & combinations. Thus, Jackson Mac Low's "vocabularies," in which the text (or score) "is a drawing, painting or collage consisting of all the words I can think of (or fit on the paper or canvas) spelled solely with the letters of one person's name," is very close in method – even, ultimately, in intention – to the first non-numerical process described above.

While numerical *gematria* & coded *temura* come easily in a language like Hebrew which is written without vowels, the possibility of similar workings in English shouldn't be discounted. The *gematria*-generated poems, above, are, however, directly translated from traditional Hebrew sources – a fact which adds to the apparent "distance & power" of the combinations, a direct relationship that 20th-century poets like Reverdy saw as the basis of the poetic image.

Chance Composition No. 1

Stick a pin through the Talmud, take the different sentences pointed to by the pin, & make them into a single discourse.

Chance Composition No. 2

Do the same for the *Zohar*.

Zohar Event
A Simultaneity for 10 or More Readers

Cut up a chapter of the *Zohar* into as many segments as there are readers.
   Distribute the cut pages, & have the readers sound their segments simultaneously.

COMMENTARY

Here the use of "chance" is limited to opening up new channels of association – as Jackson Mac Low ("The Friendship Poems"): "O blessèd chance continue to happen to me! / For I wd never plan so well – I wd have died of my planning. . . . " In a related, if trivial, process, talmudic scholars showed their erudition by sticking a pin through a volume of the Talmud, taking note only of the top word punctured, then calling out the sequence of the punctured words below.

Tristan Tzara (French, 1896 – 1963)
From MANIFESTO ON FEEBLE & BITTER LOVE

To make a dada poem
Take a newspaper.
Take a pair of scissors.
Choose an article as long as you are planning to make your poem.
Cut out the article.
Then cut out each of the words that make up this article & put them in a
     bag.
Shake it gently.
Then take out the scraps one after the other in the order in which they left
     the bag.
Copy conscientiously.
The poem will be like you.

Jackson Mac Low (b. 1922)

KADDISH GATHA

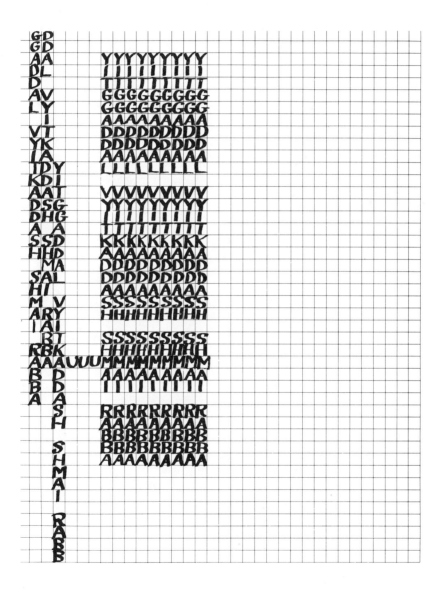

"'Kaddish Gatha' (27 April 1975) is one of an open series of performance-poem notations lettered on quadrille paper, begun early in 1961. In each Gatha chance operations have helped arrange the letters of a mantram or mantramlike prayer (here the Aramaic 'kaddish': *yitggaddal v'yitkaddash shmai rabba*, 'magnified & sanctified be His Great Name') – often, as here, so that they cross an axis of A's, U's, & M's (letters of the seed syllable *A U M*). Performers (soloists or groups) begin at any square, reading or being silent for any duration (for empty squares), 'move' to any square adjacent to its sides or corners, & thus continue till the performance ends – by spontaneous agreement, a leader's signal, or arrival at a preselected time. Letters may be read as their English names, as any sound they can stand for in any language, or grouped as syllables, words, pseudowords, word-groups, &c., formed in any direction(s). Sounds, &c., may be repeated singly or in groups, & the basic mantram or prayer may be repeated *ad lib.* (any time – any number of repetitions). Prolongable sounds may be prolonged for any duration (producing 'chords' or 'organ points' in group performances). Rhythms, pitches, &c., are chosen freely but in relation to all other sounds heard (other performers, audience, ambient sounds). 'Listen' & 'Relate' are the most important rules. Performers, guided by awareness, sensitivity, tact, courtesy, & inspiration, produce sounds or observe attentive silence thru conscious choices to modify (or not) the total situation." (J.M.L.)

*Copyright © 1978 by Jackson Mac Low. All rights reserved. Used by permission of the author.

(Hebrew, medieval)

From THE HAVDALA OF RABBI AKIBA   "A Realization"

Hear, he o that Israel, dwelleth the in Lord secret our place God, of the the
   Lord Most is High one. Shall hear, abide o under Israel, the the shadow
   Lord of our God, the Almighty. Lord is one.
Hear, I o will Israel, say the of Lord the our Lord, God, He the is Lord my
   is refuge one. And hear, my o fortress: Israel, my the God; Lord in our
   Hım God, will the I Lord trust. Is one.
Hear, surely o He Israel, shall the deliver Lord thee our from God, the the
   snare Lord of is the one. Fowler, hear, and o from Israel, the the
   noisome Lord pestilence. Our God, the Lord is one.

Hear, He o shall Israel, cover the thee Lord with our His God, feathers, the
and Lord under is His one. Wings hear, shalt o thou Israel, trust: the His
Lord truth our shall God, be the thy Lord shield is and one. Buckler.

Hear, thou o shalt Israel, not the be Lord afraid our for God the the terror
Lord by is night; one. Nor hear, for o the Israel, arrow the that Lord
flieth our by God, day; the Lord is one.

Hear, nor o for Israel, the pestilence Lord that our walketh God, in the
darkness; Lord nor is for one. The hear destruction o that Israel,
wasteth the at Lord noonday. Our God, the Lord is one.

Hear, a o thousand Israel, shall the fall Lord at our thy God, side, the and
Lord ten is thousand one. At hear, thy o right Israel, hand; the but Lord
it our shall God, not the come Lord nigh is thee. One.

Hear, only o with Israel, thine the eyes Lord shalt our thou God, behold the
and Lord see is the one. Reward hear of o the Israel, wicked. The Lord
our God, the Lord is one.

Hear, because o thou Israel hast the made Lord the our Lord, God, which
the is Lord my is refuge, one. Even hear, the o Most Israel, High, the thy
Lord habitation; our God, the Lord is one.

Hear, there o shall Israel, no the evil Lord befall our thee, God, neither the
shall Lord any is plague one. Come hear, nigh o thy Israel, dwelling.
The Lord our God, the Lord is one.

Hear, for o He Israel, shall the give Lord His our angels God, charge the
over Lord thee, is to one. Keep hear, thee o in Israel, all the thy Lord
ways. Our God, the Lord is one.

Hear, they o shall Israel, bear the thee Lord up our in God, their the hands,
Lord lest one. Thou hear, dash o thy Israel, foot the against Lord a our
stone. God, the Lord is one.

Hear, thou o shalt Israel, tread the upon Lord the our lion God, and the ad-
der: Lord the is young one. Lion hear, and o the Israel, dragon the shalt
Lord thou our trample God, under the feet. Lord is one.

Hear, because o he Israel, hath the set Lord his our love God, upon the me,
Lord therefore is will one. I hear, deliver o him: Israel, I the will Lord set
our him God, on the high, Lord because is he one. Hath hear, known o
my Israel, name. The Lord our God, the Lord is one.

Hear, he o shall Israel, call the upon Lord me, our and God, I the will Lord
answer is him: one. I hear, will o be Israel, with the him Lord our in God,
trouble; the I Lord will is deliver one. Him, hear, and o honor Israel,
him. The Lord our God, the Lord is one.

Hear, with o long Israel, life the will Lord I our satisfy God, him, the and
Lord show is him one. My hear, salvation. O Israel, the Lord our God,
the Lord is one.

J.R.

A realization of a simple collage event, in which the instructions were to alternate the words of the mantric *shema* prayer ("Hear, o Israel . . . ") with those of Psalm 91. Writes Joshua Trachtenberg: "Already in the pages of the Talmud we read that 'the demons keep away from everyone who recites the *Shema* before retiring.' There grew up an increasingly elaborate scheme of prayer around this nocturnal recitation of the *Shema* . . . coupled with potent Biblical verses and psalms." (*Jewish Magic & Superstition*, page 156.) While contemporary pieces of this sort are generally, but not invariably, more complex &/or randomized, the reader who sounds this aloud may still be aware of an intricate emergence, disappearing & interweaving of both texts.

(Hebrew / Aramaic, c. 490 A.D.)

From THE BABYLONIAN TALMUD   "The Signs"

For Memory

I

like the sand of the purple blue scorpion stirring his basket

2

All time Jordan

3

Seas   Gabriel   Hungry

4

neither exact weight nor heaped up with market officers & with a pound
three & ten NEFESH   weighs a thick strike   you shall not do
he shall not do

5

King Abraham the 10 years when he passed away he was exalted lonely

6

he who does   Deadly Poison   Enthrusts   His fellow   Broken

7

& Rabbi Yose said: Your sign for memory is TABLE IN THE NORTH & CANDELABRA IN THE SOUTH   the one increases its own & the other increases it own   there is no difficulty   THIS IS FOR US   & THAT IS FOR THEM

COMMENTARY

The Talmud, which incorporates a transcription of the older Mishna as traditional oral discourse, still preserves occasional mnemonics (*simanim* or signs): memory devices which sometimes take the form of a recombination of key words from the interchanges that follow. The results, as here, are a series of new utterances that both lead the mind back to the sources in question &, like much contemporary collage poetry, open the possibility of new readings & combinations.

(Aramaic, c. 210 A.D.)

From THE MISHNAH   "Clean & Unclean"

MISHNAH 1. IF IN A PUBLIC DOMAIN THERE WAS A DEAD CREEPING THING & A FROG, & ALSO IF THERE WAS THERE AN OLIVE'S BULK OF A CORPSE & AN OLIVE'S BULK OF CARRION, A BONE OF A CORPSE & A BONE OF CARRION, A CLOD OF CLEAN EARTH & A CLOD FROM A GRAVE AREA OR A CLOD OF CLEAN EARTH & A CLOD FROM THE LAND OF THE GENTILES, OR IF THERE WERE TWO PATHS, THE ONE UNCLEAN & THE OTHER CLEAN, & A MAN WALKED THROUGH ONE OF THEM BUT IT IS

NOT KNOWN WHICH, OR OVERSHADOWED ONE OF THEM BUT IT IS NOT KNOWN WHICH, OR HE SHIFTED ONE OF THEM BUT IT IS NOT KNOWN WHICH, RABBI AKIBA RULED THAT HE IS UNCLEAN, BUT THE SAGES RULE THAT HE IS CLEAN.

MISHNAH 2. WHETHER THE MAN SAID, "I TOUCHED AN OBJECT ON THIS SPOT BUT I DO NOT KNOW WHETHER IT WAS UNCLEAN OR CLEAN," OR "I TOUCHED ONE BUT I DO NOT KNOW WHICH OF THE TWO I TOUCHED," RABBI AKIBA RULES THAT HE IS UNCLEAN, BUT THE SAGES RULE THAT HE IS CLEAN. RABBI YOSE RULES THAT HE IS UNCLEAN IN EVERY CASE & CLEAN ONLY IN THAT OF THE PATH, SINCE IT IS THE USUAL PRACTICE FOR MEN TO GO BUT IT IS NOT THEIR USUAL PRACTICE TO TOUCH.

MISHNAH 3. IF THERE WERE TWO PATHS, THE ONE UN-CLEAN & THE OTHER CLEAN, & IF A MAN WALKED BY ONE OF THEM & THEN PREPARED CLEAN FOODSTUFFS WHICH WERE SUBSEQUENTLY CONSUMED &, HAVING BEEN SPRINKLED UPON ONCE & A SECOND TIME & HAVING PERFORMED IMMERSION & ATTAINED CLEANNESS, HE WALKED BY THE SECOND PATH & THEN PREPARED CLEAN FOODSTUFFS, THE LATTER ARE DEEMED CLEAN. IF THE FIRST FOODSTUFFS WERE STILL IN EXIS-TENCE BOTH MUST BE HELD IN SUSPENSE. IF HE HAD NOT ATTAINED CLEANNESS IN THE MEANTIME, THE FIRST ARE HELD IN SUSPENSE & THE SECOND MUST BE BURNT.

MISHNAH 4. IF THERE WAS A DEAD CREEPING THING & A FROG IN A PUBLIC DOMAIN & A MAN TOUCHED ONE OF THEM & THEN PREPARED CLEAN FOODSTUFFS WHICH WERE SUBSEQUENTLY CONSUMED, & THEN HE PERFORMED IM-MERSION, TOUCHED THE OTHER & THEN PREPARED CLEAN FOODSTUFFS, THE LATTER ARE DEEMED CLEAN. IF THE FIRST FOODSTUFFS WERE STILL IN EXISTENCE BOTH MUST BE HELD IN SUSPENSE. IF HE DID NOT PERFORM IMMERSION IN THE MEANTIME, THE FIRST ARE HELD IN SUSPENSE & THE SEC-OND MUST BE BURNT.

MISHNAH 5. IF THERE WERE TWO PATHS, THE ONE UN-CLEAN & THE OTHER CLEAN, & A MAN WALKED BY ONE OF THEM & THEN PREPARED CLEAN FOODSTUFFS, & SUBSE-QUENTLY ANOTHER MAN CAME BY & WALKED BY THE SECOND

PATH & THEN PREPARED CLEAN FOODSTUFFS, RABBI JUDAH RULED: IF EACH BY HIMSELF ASKED FOR A RULING THEY ARE BOTH TO BE DECLARED CLEAN, BUT IF THEY ASKED FOR A RULING SIMULTANEOUSLY, BOTH ARE TO BE DECLARED UNCLEAN. RABBI YOSE RULED: IN EITHER CASE THEY ARE BOTH UNCLEAN.

COMMENTARY

Babylonian Talmud, circa 5th century A.D., of which the Mishna (oral discourse) goes back to the editing & transcription by Rabbi Jehudah the Patriarch & his school, circa 200. An example of what David Antin, in relation to the "prose" of Gertrude Stein, calls "phrasal poetry," but also related to his own talking pieces, discourse out of Wittgenstein, etc. The present passage is, of course, from a much longer series, an actual discourse in which the process is one of testing, by recombinations from a set series of situations, the possibility of deriving conclusions such as *x* or not-*x*, "clean" or "not-clean," within the category of ritual purity & contamination. Note, too, that the thrust is not toward closure but a simultaneity of opposite conclusions, typified in the Talmud by the "contradictory" propositions of the schools of Hillel & Shammai, etc.: not to eliminate conflict but to recognize its presence at the heart of discourse. And if one sounds the present text as a poem – even chants it in recognition of the older practice – the sound itself assists in reconstruction of that ancient dialectic.

    Addendum. "Thought is made in the mouth." (T. Tzara.)

SOUNDING EVENTS

Sound the words as quickly as possible
Sound the words as loudly as possible
Sound the words in a whisper

Sound the words while jumping in place
Sound the words while beating your chest
Sound the words while swaying sideways

Sound the words while clapping hands
Sound the words while turning somersaults
Sound the words while standing still

Sound the words a second time
Sound the words a third time
Sound the words a fourth time

Sound the words a fifth time
Sound the words a sixth time
Sound the words a seventh time

Sound the words an eighth time
Sound the words a ninth time
Sound the words a tenth time

Sound the words a hundred times
Sound the words a thousand times
Sound the words in silence

COMMENTARY

Examples of ways in which the written text (as prayer or meditation/mantra) was brought back to the world of sound & gesture.

(1) "You will meet a company of seers coming down from the high place with a psaltery, a tambourine, a pipe, & a harp: & they will prophesy: & the spirit of Yahveh will come upon you, & you will prophesy with them, & will be turned into another man." (I Samuel 10.5 – .6.)

(2) "Prayer is copulation with the Shekinah. Just as there is swaying when copulation begins so, too, a man must sway at first & then he can remain immobile & attached to the Shekinah with great attachment. As a result of his swaying a man is able to attain a powerful stage of arousal. For he will ask himself: Why do I sway my body? Presumably it is because the Shekinah stands over against me. And as a result he will attain to a stage of great enthusiasm." (From *Tsava'at ha-Ribash,* quoted in L. Jacobs, *Hasidic Prayer.*)

(3) "He who reads without melody & repeats without song, concerning him the Scripture says: Therefore I also gave them statutes which were not to their advantage." (Rabbi Yohanan, Talmud: *Megila* 32a.)

*

A series of events & happenings – for voice & body – follow, toward conclusion of the present "book."

Word Events

Read a verse.
Read each word backwards.
Read the entire verse backwards.

Sound Event: the Silent Orchestra

Construct an orchestra made up entirely of wooden "dummy" instruments: a violin, a double bass, a trumpet, saxophone, & drum, etc. Play music in silence, while others dance to it.

COMMENTARY

"As oil is soundless / so Israel is soundless in this world." (*Canticles Raba* 1.21.)

Allan Kaprow (b. 1927)
Words: An Environment

Two rooms, one 9' × 9', leading railroad style into another, 6' × 6', each 8' high, constructed within a room. Doorways covered by white cloths.

Outside first room is a large electric sign saying "WORDS." Red and white lights blinking all around top of the walls. Inside, 4 lights hanging at eye level: a blue, a yellow, a green, and a white one, which alone blinks. Two vertical rows of lights, also not blinking, from floor to ceiling, on opposite walls. On the other two walls are five continuous rolls of cloth, also floor to ceiling, on which are stenciled words. Operated manually, these rolls, containing fixed elements, can be aligned variously with each other to make sense-groups or non-sense, as one wishes. Governing the other two walls are word strips on paper (lettered by a group of friends and myself and derived at random from a number of poetry books, newspapers, comic magazines, the telephone book, popular love stories, etc.; these having been shuffled, I composed them into wall-sized poems). Overhead, are crudely-lettered signs urging the visitors to roll the rolls, to tear off more word strips from stacks nailed to a centerpost, and to staple them over the ones already there; in addition, they are exhorted to play the victrolas and listen to the records I had made, of talk, lectures, shouts, advertisements, ramblings of nonsense, etc. – either singly or all together.

In the smaller room, painted blue, illuminated by a single, weak light

bulb and covered overhead by a plastic film, the atmosphere is very close and intimate (in contrast to the brash, open feeling of the first room). Many strips of cloth hang from the sheet of plastic filling the entire space; and above, through its filminess one can see crumpled newspapers scattered here and there on top. A visitor has to push through these hangings which brush his face like cobwebs. Clipped onto these hangings are many small pieces of paper with hand-written notes from, and to, different people. Near the doorway are a pencil, clips, and more paper for additional notes. Then, hanging all around the walls from strings are large colored chalks. (I and friends had written and drawn already on these walls to start things off and thereafter the visitors added whatever they wished.) Finally a record-player on the floor whispers when it is turned on.

This environment, therefore, is transformed every day.

Rain Event One

Whisper until it rains.

COMMENTARY

(1) The Hebrew word for magic – *kishuf* – literally "murmuring" or "muttering."

(2) "If you see a generation over whom the heavens are rust-colored like copper so that neither rain nor dew falls, it is because that generation is wanting in whisperers. What then is the remedy? Let them go to someone who knows how to whisper." (Talmud: *Ta'anit* 8a.)

(3) "In oriental countries in general, the Jews have acquired, for one reason or another, a special reputation as rainmakers." (Raphael Patai, *The Hebrew Goddess*.)

Tree Spirit Events

Then sing the trees of the wood for joy
before the Lord.

One mounts to one side.
One descends on that side.
One enters between the two.
Two crown themselves with a third.
Three enter into one.
One produces various colors.
Six of them descend on one side & six of them on the other.
Six enter into twelve.
Twelve bestir themselves to form twenty-two.
Six are comprised in ten.
Ten are fixed in one.

"... He had studied all manners of speech / even the utterance of mountains, hills & valleys / the utterance of trees & plants / the utterance of beasts & animals / He had learned them all": thus an earlier description of Hillel the Elder (first centuries B.C./A.D.), showing that reintegration with the natural world that characterizes the subterranean side of the western mystical tradition. But the obvious animism of the medieval "tree events" here given – identification of the trees of Eden with angels, etc. – combines as well with the numerology of Jewish mysticism & *poesis* (see above, pages 227ff.). Also, since numbers & letters are here identical, the reader (if acquainted with such works as Graves' *White Goddess*) may recognize a resemblance to Celtic tree alphabets, etc.

Nachman of Bratzlav (Hebrew, 1772 – 1810)
VISION EVENT

Imagine that you could constantly recall all that we know about the future world.
There is an angel with a thousand heads.
Each head has a thousand tongues.
Each tongue has a thousand voices.
Each voice has a thousand melodies.
Imagine the beauty of this angel's song.

A Scenario for Midnight

1. God enters Paradise to rejoice with the righteous.

2. All the trees in Paradise burst into hymns.

3. A wind rises from the north, a spark flies from the power of the north, God's fire, & strikes Archangel Gabriel under his wings.

4. The cry of Gabriel awakens all the cocks at midnight.

THE END OF "A BOOK OF EXTENSIONS"

Sources & Acknowledgments, &c.

The editors' transliterations of Hebrew words have proceeded wherever possible or wherever advantageous by a consistent & commonly accepted system for transcription into Roman letters. We have, however, used traditional spellings of common terms & names (Torah, Moses, Jerusalem, etc.) without regard to the systems of transcription that gave rise to them. Given the existence of alternative systems of transliteration, we have also maintained to the letter any transcriptions occurring inside texts by other translators reproduced here.

PAGE 3
"Rabbi Eliezer said." Translation by J. R. & H. L. from Babylonian Talmud: *Berakhot* 28b, 29b. Compare Ezra Pound (Canto 53):

> Tching prayed on the mountain and
> wrote MAKE IT NEW
> on his bath tub
> Day by day make it new

PAGE 15
"Question / Answer." From Irving A. Agus, *Rabbi Meir of Rothenburg* (K T A V Publishing House, New York, 1970), page 190.

"I form the light." Isaiah 45.7.

PAGE 17
"The First, the Last." After translation of 4 Esdras in R. H. Charles, *Apocrypha & Pseudepigrapha of the Old Testament* (Clarendon Press, Oxford, 1913), volume 1, page 574. A Latin text, c. 3rd or 4th century A.D., from a Greek original, c. 2nd century A.D., & even earlier Hebrew. The original Ezra, "the scribe," led the return from Babylonia in 458 B.C.; this is Ezra "the apocalyptist."

PAGE 18
"The Greater Hekhalot." Adapted from the Hebrew & the English translation in Gershom Scholem, *Jewish Gnosticism, Merkabah Mysticism, & Talmudic Tradition* (Jewish Theological Seminary of America, New York, 1960), pages 59–60.

PAGE 19
"Elya." From E. Jabès, *Elya* (Tree Books, Berkeley, California, 1974), page 72. Born in Cairo, Jabès has lived in Paris since 1956.

PAGE 20
"The Great Holy Assembly." From Roy A. Rosenberg, *The Anatomy of God* (K T A V Publishing House, New York, 1973), pages 104–5. "The Great Holy Assembly (*Idra Raba*) is a discrete section of the *Zohar* ([Book of] Splendor), a 13th-century assemblage by Moses de

Leon but claiming to go back to the circle of Simeon bar Yoḥai (see page 123). Used by permission of K T A V Publishing House, Inc. Copyright © 1973 by Roy A. Rosenberg.

PAGE 21

"Sefer Raziel." From *The Book of Noah* (Tree Books, Berkeley, California, 1975), after Johann Maier's version from the original Hebrew. "This is a Book out of the Books of Mystery given to Noah the son of Lamech . . . by the Angel Raziel in the Year of his entry into the Ark, at its doorway."

PAGE 22

"A Poem for the Sefirot as a Wheel of Light." Direct translation from *Sefer Emek ha-Melekh* [Book of the Valley of the King] (Amsterdam 1648) & reprint in *Encyclopedia Judaica*, volume 10, pages 597–98.

PAGE 26

"1st Light Poem." From J. Mac Low, *22 Light Poems* (Black Sparrow Press, Los Angeles, 1968).

PAGE 27

"Sh'iur Koma." From *Merkava Shlema* (Jerusalem, 1921), a miscellany of texts from the manuscript collection of Solomon Musajoff. Based largely on the physical description of the "divine lover" in the Song of Songs.

PAGE 29

"For the Beard of the Great Face." Reprinted in *Encyclopedia Judaica*, volume 10, page 544.

PAGE 31

"A Poem for the Small Face." Translated with the assistance of Yerachmiel Weinstein from the Sefardic prayerbook. Luria – also known as *ha-Ari*, or "the lion" – was one of the pivotal kabbalist poets & mythmakers. Leader of an esoteric circle in Safed, his workings were oral, & the later writing down was by disciples such as Ḥayim Vital. "Before Luria's theoretical teachings became known, he won fame as a poet." (G. Scholem, *Kabbalah*, page 426.)

PAGE 33

"A Poem for the Shekinah on the Feast of the Sabbath." From J. Rothenberg, *Poland/1931* (New Directions, New York, 1974), after a translation in Gershom Scholem's *On the Kabbalah & Its Symbolism*. A companion piece to the preceding.

PAGE 37

"The Greater Hekhalot." J. R.'s working from Hebrew & translation in Gershom Scholem, *Jewish Gnosticism, Merkabah Mysticism, & Talmudic Tradition* (Jewish Theological Seminary of America, New York, 1960), page 32.

PAGE 39

"Angel." Translation from the text in T. Tzara, *Oeuvres Complètes* (Flammarion, Paris, 1975), page 198. Tzara, born Samuel Rosenstock in Moinesti, Rumania, came to Zurich, circa 1916, to found Dada. From Paris & elsewhere thereafter, he was a key figure in the Surrealist revolution, etc. "between the wars."

PAGE 40

"The Book of the Left Pillar." Direct translation from the text of *Sefer Amud ha-Smoli* in Gershom Scholem, "Le-Heker Kabbalat R. Yitsḥak ben R. Ya'akov Ha-Kohen," *Tarbiz* IV (1933).

PAGE 42

"Hero/Lil." From D. Meltzer, *Hero/Lil* (Black Sparrow Press, Los Angeles, 1973).

PAGE 46

"The Book Bahir." Direct translation from Reuven Margoliot's definitive edition (Jerusalem, 1951) of *Sefer ha-Bahir.*

PAGE 47

"The 'Who?' of ibn Abitur." Translation from Hebrew text in Hayim Schirmann (ed.), *Ha-Shira ha-Ivrit bi-Sfarad u-vi-Frovence* (Jerusalem / Tel Aviv, 1954), page 56. First of the "new poets" of medieval Spain but still heavily into the earlier *piyut* practice – as in the acrostic (alphabet & poet's name) translated here as such. The pronoun "who," like other pronouns (see above, page 59), was itself thought of as a name of God.

PAGE 51

"The Withdrawal, the Exile." From J. Gikatilla, *Ginat Egoz* (1274): an introduction to alphabet & number mysticism, etc., his earliest surviving work. Born in Castille, lived many years in Segovia; a student of Abraham Abulafia & acquaintance, circa 1280, of Moses de Leon, author of the *Zohar.*

PAGE 52

"The Torah of the Void." Translation from *Likutei Maharan* 1.64, in *Tree* 4 (Berkeley, California, 1974), condensed by the present editor. A great-grandson of the Baal Shem Tov (see above, page 148), Nachman's brand of hasidism involved a system of solitary meditation called *hisbodidus (hitbodedut)* – practiced at times as a virtual return to forest & wilderness. In addition, a stress on story-telling &, as here, music as means to enlightenment; thus "in the high spheres there exist temples that can be opened through song only."

PAGE 59

"Nothing." For Gikatilla, see above.

PAGE 60

"Fragment." From F. Kafka, *Dearest Father* (Shocken Books, New York, 1954), page 303. Copyright © 1954 by Shocken Books, Inc.

PAGE 61

"The Book of Formation." Lenowitz's translation (at center) of the opening segment of the *Sefer Yetsira* – the surrounding commentaries, from the 9th through 18th centuries, arranged according to the standard Hebrew practice.

PAGE 63

"The Ten Words of Creation." Samaritan Hebrew script from James A. Montgomery, *The Samaritans: The Earliest Jewish Sect* (1907), pages 272, 274. "It is too often and too easily forgotten ... that in speaking of Samaritans we are of speaking of heretical Judaism." (G. Scholem, *Jewish Gnosticism*, etc., page 4.)

PAGE 63

"Variations on Genesis." (1) From *The Baraita of the Work of Creation*, translation by Jack Hirschman in *Tree* 2 (Bolinas, California, 1971), page 54. (2) J. R.'s working after translation in M. Simon & H. Sperling (eds.), *The Zohar* (The Soncino Press, London, 1934), volume 1, page 63. (3) Translation of Genesis 1.1 – .5, in Doria & Lenowitz, *Origins* (Anchor Books, New York, 1976), page 37.

PAGE 65

"The Pirke de Rabbi Eliezer." From J. Rothenberg, *The Pirke & the Pearl* (Tree Books, Berkeley, 1974), after a translation in Gerald Friedlander, *The Pirke de Rabbi Eliezer* (London, 1916), pages 15–16. The *pirke* (i.e. "chapters") go back, by way of reputation, to Eliezer-the-Great ben Hyrkanos, who lived circa A.D. 150, "was known for his great erudition . . . but was ultimately excommunicated."

PAGE 65

"A Prologue to the Elements of Creation." From M. Simon & H. Sperling (eds.), *The Zohar*, op. cit., volume 3, page 80.

PAGE 66

"Fire-Poem." Direct translation from M. Zulay (ed.), *Piyutei Yannai* (1938). Yannai was one of the first known *paytanim* (from the Greek, *poëtēs*), makers of a kind of poetry called *piyut:* "compositions added to . . . the ancient prayers [of the synagogue] . . . to constitute – in contrast to the stable and stationary standard prayers – an ever-changing and restless element within the Jewish liturgy . . . that was responsible for the development within Judaism of about half a hundred different rites" (Shalom Spiegel).

PAGE 67

"Water-Poem." Direct translation from the Hebrew prayer book of the rain prayer (*piyut*) chanted on the eighth day of *Sukot* (Tabernacles) for the *musaf* service. Like Yannai (see preceding), Kallir was an early *paytan* & a greatly prolific poet (above, page 193).

PAGE 71

"The Book of Mysteries." Direct translation from Mordecai Margalioth (ed.), *Sefer ha-Razim* (American Academy for Jewish Research, Jerusalem, 1966), pages 96–100. "A newly recovered book of magic from the Talmudic period . . . collected from *geniza* fragments and other sources."

PAGE 74

"The Code of Day & Night." Working after J. M. Allegro, "An Astrological Cryptic Document from Qumran," *Journal of Semitic Studies*, volume 9 (1964), pages 291–94. Dead Sea Scroll materials.

PAGE 76

"Menorah." Arranged by J. R. from E. R. Goodenough, *Jewish Symbols in the Greco-Roman Period* (Pantheon Books, New York, 1953), volume 4, pages 92ff: a discussion of menorah/tree-of-life in the *Zohar*, etc.

PAGE 77

"Serpent." For more on Nathan of Gaza, the prophet of the "heretical" 17th-century messiah Sabbatai Zevi, see above, page 138. The poem as *gematria* (page 232) turns up in Scholem's biography of Sabbatai Zevi & many other sources.

PAGE 78

"The Wind   Two Trees   Men and Women." From *Tree* 5 (Berkeley, California, 1975), pages 8–9. "The form is modelled on the standard presentation of text and commentary in Hebrew religious books."

PAGE 80

"The Iyyob Translation." From Zukofsky's contemporary masterpiece, *A* (University of

California Press, 1978) – the opening of the 15th section a translation-by-sound from the Hebrew Book of Job, principally the whirlwind sections of Chapter 38. A counterpointing & close imitation of the source language, or post-Joycean attempt to deliver meaning by pun & rhythm. Copyright © 1978 by Celia & Louis Zukofsky.

PAGE 83

"Nothing, only an image." From F. Kafka, *Dearest Father* (Schocken Books, New York, 1954), pages 313, 261.

PAGE 83

"If you are 'my witnesses.'" As quoted in *Pesikta de Rav Kahana* 102b.

PAGE 85

"Patriarchal Poetry." From G. Stein, *Bee Time Vine* (Yale University Press, New Haven, 1953), page 263. ". . . There are all these emotions lying around; no reason why we shouldn't use them." Copyright © 1953 by Alice B. Toklas.

PAGE 88

"Akeda." Center text: Genesis 22.1 – .19; surrounding commentary from the *Sefer Ha'agada*, eds. Bialik, Rawnitsky.

PAGE 88

"The Testaments of the 12 Patriarchs." Working after translation in M. Gaster, *Studies & Texts* (KTAV Publishing House, New York, 1928, 1971), volume 1, page 81. "This is the will (testament) of Naphtali, son of Jacob."

PAGE 91

"A Prologue to the Works of Moses." From "The Revelation of Moses" in ibid., page 126.

PAGE 91

"The Image of Speech at Sinai." Direct translation from Eleazar ben Judah of Worms, *Sodei Razaya* [Secrets of Secrets] (ed. Kamelhar, Bilgoraj. Poland, 1936), page 43. "*I have seen the eternal interior, not ocular vision. . . . I have spoken to the prophets; I have multiplied the visions & through the intermediation of prophets, I have pointed out appearances.*" (Eleazar of Worms, "The Book of Prophecy.")

PAGE 92

"The Book of Exodus." Direct translation from Exodus 15.1 – .21, one of the oldest documents in the Bible, from the very beginnings of the Yahvist cult in Israel.

PAGE 95

"The First Book of Samuel." Translation & working from I Samuel 28.3 – .14 (the "Samuel strain"), with assistance on the varieties of Jewish shamanism from Arvid S. Kapelrud, "Shamanistic Features in the Old Testament," in Carl-Martin Edsman (ed.), *Studies in Shamanism* (Scripta Instituti Donneriani Aboensis, 1967). An Israelite judge & prophet, Samuel lived in the 10th century B.C. & was involved with Saul & David in "the transition from a loose confederation of Hebrew tribes to a centralized monarchy" (*Encyclopedia Judaica*) – hence the elimination of the more free-wheeling shamanistic practices. (N.B. The "shaman" [*mekhashefa*] of the third commentary, above, is feminine, a word usually translated as "witch" or "sorceress," but clearly tied to the aboriginal religion; cf. Babylonian *kassapu* = darkness, privacy, cutting [of the self, of the entrails].)

PAGE 97

"A Vision in the Voice of Yahveh." Direct translation from Amos 8.1 – .12. "I am no prophet, nor a prophet's son; but I am a herdsman & a dresser of sycamore trees, & the Lord took me from following the flock, & the Lord said to me, Go, prophesy to my people Israel." (Amos 7.14 – .15.)

PAGE 99

"Psalm 137." Direct translation from the Hebrew.

PAGE 101

"Elijah & the Priests of Baal." Direct translation from I Kings 18. An extreme Yahvist of the 9th century B.C. & later legendary hero, central to the messianic myths, etc.

PAGE 107

"A Poem About Ashera." Translation based on C. Gordon, *Ugaritic Textbook* (Ventnor Publications, Ventnor, New Jersey, 1965), Text 51, in H. Lenowitz, *A Reasonable Proposal for the Translation of Ugaritic Mythopoetry* (dissertation, University of Texas, 1971), pages 52 – 54.

PAGE 110

"The Alphabet of Ben Sira." Direct translation from *Alfabeta de-ben Sira* (Warsaw, 1927), Version One.

PAGE 114

"A Poem for the High Priest." Direct translation from the Yom Kippur prayer book, with the assistance of Yerachmiel Weinstein. The poem occurs in the Yom Kippur service at the time of the priestly benediction, its deeper source the description of the High Priest Simon in the Wisdom of Ben Sira (c. 170 B.C.).

PAGE 116

"The Acts of Saint John." J. R.'s redaction &/or working, based on versions by Edgar Hennecke, Max Pulver, & G. R. S. Mead from the gnostic Acts of Saint John.

PAGE 121

"A Poem for Bar Yohai." Direct translation from the *Tikum Shabat* ceremony of the Sephardic rite.

PAGE 124

"The Great Lament." From the Talmud: *Mo'ed Katan* 25b, as cited in Emanuel Feldman, "The Rabbinic Lament," in *Jewish Quarterly Review*, volume 63, number 1 (July 1972), page 72.

PAGE 125

"I Am the Babe of Joseph Stalin's Daughter." From R. Owens, *I Am the Babe of Joseph Stalin's Daughter* (The Kulchur Foundation, New York, 1972). *Din* ("judgment") is an alternative term for the sefira *gevura* (see above, page 24). "In her book . . . one aspect of the kabbalistic system dominates: the sefira called DIN; more generally, the left side of God." (H. Lenowitz, "Din & Razel," in *Margins*, number 24, page 84.)

PAGE 126

"The Prophecy of Jesus ben Hananiah." From Flavius Josephus, *The Wars of the Jews*, 6.301.

PAGE 127

"Toldot Yeshu." Translation & working after Hugh J. Schonfeld, *According to the Hebrews*

(Duckworth, London, 1937), with additions from the Strasburg manuscript (*Ma'ase Yeshu ha-Notsri*) in Samuel Krauss, *Das Leben Jesus nach jüdischen Quellen* (Berlin, 1902).

PAGE 129

"The Withdrawal of the Shekinah." From Raphael Patai, *The Hebrew Goddess* (K T A V Publishing House, New York, 1967), page 143.

PAGE 130

"A Curse & Angry Poem Against the Nations." From the Passover Hagada; the "poem" here is the opening of Psalm 115.

PAGE 131

"Midrash of the Absent" (*Midrash ha-Ne'elam*). Direct translation of "The Palace of Splendor & the Bird's Nest" from "The Book of the Ways of Life, called The Testimony of Rabbi Eliezer the Great," in Yehuda Even-Shmuel (ed.), *Midreshei Ge'ula* (Mosad Bialik, Jerusalem/Tel Aviv, 1968), pages 309–10. "This section of the Testimony of Eliezer the Great is in fact a portion of the *Midrash ha-Ne'elam*" (esoteric or concealed commentary), a series of writings that form the earliest layer of the *Zohar*.

PAGE 133

"How He Went as Messiah." Direct translation from A. Abulafia, *Sefer ha-Eydut* after text in G. Scholem, *Ha-Kabala shel Sefer ha-Tmuna v'shel Avraham Abulafia* (Akademon, Jerusalem, 1968), page 197.

PAGE 134

"The Rainbow Calendar of Isaac Luria." Direct translation from *Sefer Simanei Ra'ashim ve-Ra'amim ve-Likui ha-Me'orot* [Book of the Signs of Earthquakes, Thunders, & Eclipses] (Lemburg, 1848).

PAGE 136

"'1648': For Cossacks." Direct translation from Yiddish text in Ruth Rubin, *Voices of a People: The Story of Yiddish Folk Song* (McGraw-Hill, New York, 1973), pages 200–2.

PAGE 137

"The Vision of Rabbi Abraham." Adapted from a translation in Gershom Scholem, *Sabbatai Sevi* (Princeton University Press, Princeton, New Jersey, 1973), pages 224–26.

PAGE 139

"3 Poems for Sabbatai Zevi." Direct translations from Ladino & Hebrew in M. Attias & G. Scholem, *Songs & Hymns of the Sabbateans* (Tel Aviv, 1948), pages 136, 172, 123, 180, & 88.

PAGE 141

"The Song of the Sexton." Cited also in Abraham J. Heschel, *The Earth Is the Lord's* (Henry Schuman, New York, 1950), page 48.

PAGE 142

"The Book of the Sayings of the Lord." Previously unpublished translations from Frank's *Ksiega Słów Panskich* (Book of the Sayings of the Lord), based on texts in the Hebrew edition of A. Kraushar's *Frank & His Following* ("original" in Polish; Hebrew translation by N. Sokolow).

PAGE 147

"Five for the Rebbe." Direct translation of Yiddish texts in R. Rubin, op. cit., passim.

PAGE 149

"Poor People." From I. Howe & E. Greenberg (eds.), *A Treasury of Yiddish Poetry* (Holt, Rinehart & Winston, New York, 1969), page 230.

PAGE 149

"Zaritsky's Children." Direct translations from Yiddish texts in R. Rubin, op. cit. Zaritsky's cigarette factory was in Cherkassy, near Kiev. The quote at the end is from the Talmud: *Hagiga* 9b.

PAGE 151

"Two Poems." From I Howe & E Greenberg, *A Treasury*, pages 180–82. Born in Volhynia & later resident in Paris, Markish returned to the U.S.S.R. in 1926. Arrested in 1948, executed 1952.

PAGE 153

"Good Night, World." From Ruth Whitman (ed.), *The Selected Poems of Jacob Glatstein* (October House, New York, 1972), pages 59–60. Born in Lublin, Poland, Glatstein emigrated to the U.S.A. in 1914: American & Yiddish.

PAGE 155

"A Death Fugue." From J. Rothenberg (ed.), *New Young German Poets* (City Lights Books, San Francisco, 1959), pages 16–17. Celan's parents were killed in a German death camp, which he survived to become the first great postwar poet in the German language; later an exile & a suicide:

We were, we are, we shall remain
a Nothing,
blooming:
the Nothing-, the
No-man's-Rose.

PAGE 156

"God in Europe." From R. Mezey (ed.), *Poems from the Hebrew* (Thomas Y. Crowell, New York, 1973), pages 98–99. Born in eastern Galicia & resident from 1924 in Israel.

PAGE 157

"National Thoughts." From Y. Amichai, *Selected Poems* (Penguin Books, Middlesex, England, 1971), page 64. Reprinted by permission of Jonathan Cape Ltd. (London, England).

PAGE 158

"Jaweh and Allah Battle." From *The Holy Beggars' Gazette* (San Francisco, 1975), Winter-Spring issue, pages 22–27.

PAGE 160

"Terror." From Jerome Rothenberg, *That Dada Strain* (New Directions, New York, 1983), page 64.

PAGE 164

"Semite." From G. Oppen, *Collected Poems* (New Directions, New York, 1974), pages 246–47. Copyright 1972, 1974 by George Oppen. Reprinted by permission of New Directions Publishing Corp.

PAGE 169

"The Gezer Calendar." From *Inscriptions Reveal: Documents from the Time of the Bible, the Mishna & the Talmud* (Israel Museum, Jerusalem, 1973), page 8.

PAGE 170

"Y H V H's Battle with the Serpent." From H. Lenowitz & C. Doria (eds.), *Origins* (Anchor Books, New York, 1975), pages 289–90: Lenowitz's translations of Isaiah 51.9 – .10, Job 26.12 – .13, & Psalm 74.13 – .17.

PAGE 171

"The Song of Deborah." Direct translation from Judges 5.

PAGE 175

"The Song of Songs." J. R.'s working, after various translations of verses from the Song of Solomon 5.

PAGE 178

"The Maiden." J. R.'s working, after various English versions, but especially that of R. McL. Wilson in Edgar Hennecke, *New Testament Apocrypha* (The Westminster Press, Philadelphia, 1964), volume 2, pages 445 – 46.

PAGE 180

"A Charm Against Lilith." From the Hebrew text in G. Scholem, *Jewish Gnosticism, Merkabah Mysticism, & Talmudic Tradition* (Jewish Theological Seminary of America, New York, 1960), page 73.

PAGE 181

"The Evil Eye (The Good Eye) Einehore." From *Alcheringa*, old series (New York, 1973), number 5, pages 71 – 76; based on interviews with ten Yiddish-speaking informants in Toronto & Regina Lilienthal's "classic article" in *Yidishe Filologye* (1924).

PAGE 183

"Children's Rain Songs." From French translation in Louis Brunot & Elie Malka, *Textes Judéo-Arabes de Fès* (Institut des Hautes Études Marocaines, Rabat, 1939), page 305.

PAGE 184

"Bride's Song Against Demons." J. R.'s working, after translation in Johanna Spector, "Bridal Songs & Ceremonies from San'a, Yemen," from R. Patai, F. L. Utley, & D. Noy (eds.), *Studies in Biblical & Jewish Folklore* (Indiana University Press, Bloomington, 1960), page 257.

PAGE 185

"The Thief's Play." Direct translation from Yiddish text in Noah Priluzky & Samuel Lehman, *Studies in Yiddish Philology, Literature & Ethnology* (Warsaw, 1926–33), volume 1, pages 287 – 90.

PAGE 188

"Lullaby a Story." J. R.'s translation from the oral tradition.

PAGE 189

"A Calendar: The Year of the Messiah." Direct translation of text in Yehuda Even-Shmuel (ed.), *Midreshei Ge'ula* (Mosad Bialik, Jerusalem/Tel Aviv, 1968), pages 113–16.

"Piyut: 'A Great Music.'" Direct translation from text in Hayim Schirmann, *Shirim Hadashim min ha-Geniza* (Jerusalem, 1966), page 57. The *piyut* (see above, page 254) works off a single end rhyme & an acrostic, *Alvan Hazan Hazak* (= Alvan, the singer, be strong).

"Three Love Poems." Direct translations from text in H. Schirmann (ed.), *Ha-Shira ha-Ivrit bi-Sfarad u-vi Frovence* (Jerusalem/Tel Aviv, 1954), volume 1, pages 168, 167, 154. Ha-Nagid – Isma'il ibn Nagrela in Arabic – was vizier to the King of Granada & for 18 years commander of his armies. He was one of the first in whom a strong influence of Arabic literary modalities opened up new possibilities of form & content, though such Arab influence is hardly needed to explain the homosexual presence, etc., here & elsewhere.

"The 16-Year-Old Poet." Direct translation from H. Schirmann (ed.), ibid., page 192.

"Constellations." The 22nd section of Gabirol's long poem, *Keter Malkhut*, the title of which names the first & last of the *sefirot* (above, page 24), thus pointing to a possible kabbalistic reading of the work. Related as well to his philosophical treatise, *Mekor Hayim* (The Source of Life). His country: Spain.

"From Jehudah Halevi's Songs to Zion." From C. Reznikoff, *By the Waters of Manhattan* (New Directions, New York, 1962), pages 92 – 93. Active in Spain during a time of Muslim-Christian conflict, Ha-Levi left there en route to the Holy Land & likely died in Egypt. But legend has it "that he managed to reach the city of Jerusalem, and, as he kissed its stones, a passing Arab horseman . . . trampled on him just as he was reciting his elegy, 'Zion, do you ask if the captives are at peace?'" (*Encyclopedia Judaica.*) Copyright © 1959 by Charles Reznikoff. Reprinted by permission of New Directions Publishing Corp.

"I Have a Garment." From R. Mezey (ed.), *Poems from the Hebrew* (Thomas Y. Crowell Company, New York, 1973), page 65. A poet, grammarian, biblical commentator, philosopher, astronomer, physician, Abraham ibn Ezra was probably the most innovative of the Spanish Hebrew poets, working at times with shaped poems, mixed languages, letters, riddles, epigrams, etc.

"Proensa." G. E.'s working based on a translation in Israel Zinberg, *A History of Jewish Literature* (Case Western Reserve University, Cleveland, 1972), volume 2, pages 99 – 100. Touched by the surrounding *poesis* of Provence, he was "a kind of Jewish troubador who made the rounds of the communities with his musical instruments, as he himself states in some of his poems." (Don Pagis, in *Encyclopedia Judaica*, volume 13, page 689.)

"Italian Sonnet." G. E.'s working based on a translation in ibid., page 209. Manoello Giudeo in Italian, he wrote a long visionary poem, *Mahberet ha-Tofet ve-ha-Eden*, a journey to Hell & Paradise modelled on that of Dante. He also worked, as here, in Italian; introduced the Petrarchan sonnet into Hebrew.

PAGE 200

"Stone of Choice." R. O.'s working based on a translation in ibid., page 224. Born in Provence, Kalonymos (called Maestro Calo) was active mostly in Italy as a poet & parodist. The quote that ends this poem is from the morning prayer service.

PAGE 202

"The Castle." J. R.'s working based on a translation in Jes P. Asmussen, *Studies in Judeo-Persian Literature* (E. J. Brill, Leiden, 1973) of Sahin's "Epic of King Kishvar." The name Kishvar (literally "region" or "country") is probably made up, & the work shares the fantastic side of Persian *poesis*, of which it is in fact a part. Sahin's own name means "the falcon."

PAGE 203

"Children of the Times." Previously unpublished working based on an earlier translation into German. Najara was born in Damascus & was associated with Luria's kabbalists in Safed; the Sabbateans later took him as a messianic prophet.

PAGE 205

"The Book of the Letter." Translation from *Sefer ha-Ot* in *Tree* 1 (Bolinas, California, 1970), pages 145–46. For more on Abulafia, see pages 133, 219.

PAGE 206

"The Eighth or Hidden Sacred Book of Moses." From Hans Dieter Betz, *The Greek Magical Papyri in Translation* (University of Chicago Press, 1986), pages 191–93. Copyright © 1986 by The University of Chicago.

PAGE 209

"Lock Your Heart That It May Not Brood." Gach's working after text in I. Zinberg, *A History of Jewish Literature* (Case Western Reserve University Press, Cleveland, 1972), volume two. Sometimes spoken of as "father of the Kabbalah," Isaac the Blind was the first kabbalist to devote his work entirely to mysticism, building on the symbolism of *Sefer ha-Bahir* (above, page 47), with whose authorship he's sometimes credited. A "language mystic" of the first order, he may have coined the term *Ein-Sof* (the "infinite" or "endless") as designation for the Hidden God.

PAGE 210

"The Garden of Pomegranates." From Moses Cordovero's *Pardes Rimonim*, the work of the outstanding kabbalist of Safed before Isaac Luria.

PAGE 211

"Concrete Poem." Translation from "Samaritan Phylacteries & Amulets" (Hebrew text) in Moses Gaster, *Studies & Texts* (KTAV Publishing House, New York, 1928, 1971), volume 3, page 128.

PAGE 212

"Composition Around the Ineffable Name." From manuscript of Moses Cordovero, *Pardes Rimonim* ("The Garden of Pomegranates") in the Bibliothèque National, Paris.

PAGE 213

"Name Event One." From description in R. Patai, F. L. Utley, & D. Noy (eds.), "Two Remedy Books in Yiddish from 1474 & 1508," in *Studies in Biblical & Jewish Folklore* (Indiana University Press, Bloomington, 1960), pages 294–95.

PAGE 213

"Name Event Two." From description in Joshua Trachtenberg, *Jewish Magic & Superstition* (Atheneum, New York, 1939, 1970), page 83.

PAGE 214

"Life of the World to Come." Direct translation from one of several manuscripts of *Hayei ha-Olam ha-Ba* in the British Museum; the work is sometimes called *Sefer ha-Igulim*, "The Book of Circles."

PAGE 220

"Image of the Wall." From *Tree* 5 (Berkeley, California, 1975), page 210. A California artist & major collagist. "In Wallace Berman's shack in Beverly Glen, I first encountered a then 'hip' american work combining a turned-on sensibility with Hebrew letters. Berman later was to develop this through collagic-dada sensibilities and make use of Hebrew letters within the photoplay submissive to the 'earth' of southern california." (Jack Hirschman.)

PAGE 221

"The Masora Calligrams." From various medieval manuscripts, as reproduced in Berjouhi Bowler, "The Word As Ikon," *Typographica* 8 (London, 1968).

PAGE 224

"Calligram." From T. Tzara, *Oeuvres Complètes* (Flammarion, Paris, 1975), volume 1, page 522.

PAGE 225

"Celestial Alphabet Event." From J. Gaffarel, *Curiosités innoviés* (1637), in Kurt Seligmann, *The Mirror of Magic* (Pantheon Books, New York, 1948), page 330.

PAGE 226

"The 10 Sefirot As a Labyrinth of Letters." From Moses Cordovero, *Pardes Rimonim* ("The Garden of Pomegranates"), in the Bibliothèque National, Paris.

PAGE 227

"The Numbers." From *Encyclopedia Judaica*, volume 2, page 546.

PAGE 228

"A Talisman for Venus." From Idries Shah, *The Secret Lore of Magic* (The Citadel Press, New York, 1958), page 293.

PAGE 229

"A Number Blessing." From C. Morrow, *A Book of Numbers*, unpublished manuscript of compositions based on simple counting.

PAGE 230

"25 Gematria." Mostly traditional examples of gematria, from J. Rothenberg & H. Lenowitz, *Gematria 27* (Membrane Press, Milwaukee, 1977).

PAGE 233

"Chance Compositions." From a description in Herbert Weiner, *9½ Mystics: The Kabbala Today* (The Macmillan Company, New York, 1969), page 80.

PAGE 234

"Zohar Event." From a discussion with Alan D. Corré concerning some Sephardic Jewish prayer practices & the simultaneities of Jackson Mac Low.

PAGE 234

"Manifesto on Feeble & Bitter Love." From *Dada manifeste sur l'amour faible et l'amour amer,* read at the Galerie Povolozky, Paris, December 9, 1920, & reprinted many times elsewhere. For more on Tzara, see above, page 252.

PAGE 235

"Kaddish Gatha." Previously unpublished poem. Commissioned for *A Big Jewish Book.*

PAGE 236

"The Havdala of Rabbi Akiba." The poem, previously unpublished, follows instructions in the medieval text (see Commentary), which does not include a realization *per se.* The 91st Psalm, used here, was particularly effective against demons.

PAGE 238

"The Babylonian Talmud." Assembled from I. Epstein (ed.), *The Babylonian Talmud* (Soncino Press, London), especially volume 4, part 2: *Baba Batra.*

PAGE 239

"The Mishnah." From I. Epstein (ed.), *The Babylonian Talmud: Tohorot* (Soncino Press, London), volume 5, pages 385–87.

PAGE 241

"Sounding Events." Multiple sources & observations – & the suggestion per Harris Lenowitz that the fast reading of prayers in synagogues etc. is in fact a kind of speed mantra.

PAGE 243

"Word Events." From description in J. Trachtenberg, *Jewish Magic & Superstition* (Atheneum, New York, 1939, 1970), page 111.

PAGE 243

"Sound Event: The Silent Orchestra." From description in Herbert Weiner, *9½ Mystics* (The Macmillan Company, New York, 1969), page 151.

PAGE 243

"Words." Photos from A. Kaprow. *Assemblages, Environments, & Happenings* (Harry Abrams, New York, 1966), from an environmental happening at the Smolin Gallery, New York, 1962.

PAGE 247

"Rain Event One." From multiple sources, e.g., those in the commentary; the connection to "murmuring, muttering" from *The Friday Night Book* (Soncino Press, London, 1933). "Said Rabbi Eleazar ben Perata: Ever since the Temple was destroyed, rain is diminishing in the world." (Talmud: *Ta'anit* 19b.)

PAGE 247

"Tree Spirit Events." Based on H. Sperling & M. Simon (eds.), *The Zohar* (Soncino Press, London, 1934), volume 1, page 261.

PAGE 248

"Vision Event." Based on Nathan of Nemirov, *Rabbi Nachman's Wisdom* [*Shevachay Ha-Ran*] (Leonard M. Kaplan, Brooklyn, 1973), page 222. But, adds Nachman, "... if you could imagine such things without forgetting ... comparing your own limited abilities to the immensity of such a being ... it would be utterly impossible for you to endure life.... You would die before your time."

PAGE 249

"A Scenario at Midnight." From description in Gershom Scholem, *On the Kabbalah & Its Symbolism* (Schocken Books, New York, 1965), page 147. A mythologized version of a midnight ritual (*tikun hatsot*) "in which the exile of the *Shekhina* is dramatized & lamented. . . . At midnight the *Shekhina* . . . sings songs & hymns to her spouse . . . & a dialogue or even a *hieros gamos* [sacred marriage] is enacted between God & the *Shekhina.*" (See above, page 36.)

Would to God that all the Lords people
were Prophets
Numbers XI. ch 29 v.

חזק חזק ונתחזק
ḤAZAK ḤAZAK VENITḤAZEK
Strong Strong we make ourselves Strong

14 Sivan 5749
the day called "hand"

THIS IS THE END OF "EXILED IN THE WORD"